MYSTERY RELIGIONS
IN THE ANCIENT WORLD

JOSCELYN GODWIN

MYSTERY RELIGIONS

IN THE ANCIENT WORLD

HARPER & ROW, PUBLISHERS, San Francisco
Cambridge, Hagerstown, New York, Philadelphia,
London, Mexico City, São Paulo, Sydney
1817

Acknowledgments

The author is grateful to Jill Purce for helping to
conceive the idea of this book, and for her ever
discerning criticism; to Jane Powell, for
inspiration en route; and to Janet Godwin, for
helping him to finish it. He also thanks his
colleagues at Colgate University, particularly
William Skelton and Dexter Morrill, for their
kindly encouragement of his broader interests,
and for material assistance from the Humanities
Faculty Development Fund.

General Editor: Jill Purce

FIRST U.S. EDITION

Printed in Great Britain

LC: 81-47423

ISBN: 0-06-063 1406

81 82 83 84 85 10 9 8 7 6 5 4 3 2 1

Contents

Introduction   7

Chapters

MOMUS: Tell, me, O Zeus, however did Attis, and Corybas, and Sabazius ever get trundled in upon us? Or Mithras over there, the Mede, in his caftan and cap, who doesn't even speak Greek? And you, too, dog-faced Anubis – how do you think you'll pass for a god if you keep barking? I'm ashamed, Zeus, to mention all the ibises, monkeys, billy-goats and worse beasts still, which have somehow been smuggled out of Egypt into Heaven. However can you bear it, Gods, to see them worshipped as much as yourselves, or even more? And you, Zeus, how can you put up with those rams' horns they stick on your head?

ZEUS: All these points you mention about the Egyptians are in truth unseemly. Nevertheless, Momus, most of them are matters of symbolism; and one who is not an adept in the Mysteries really should not laugh at them.

(Lucian, *The Parliament of Gods* 9–11)

Introduction

An extraordinary variety of paths was open to the Mediterranean and European peoples in the last centuries before, and the first centuries after Christ. The subjects of the Roman Empire enjoyed a freedom of choice in religious matters unparalleled until modern times. The similarity goes further: so far, indeed, that it seems almost as though the present epoch is an accelerated recapitulation of the earlier one. In such a case it is possible to use past history as a lens through which to view more clearly our own age – and vice versa. In both epochs we see the old religions degenerating through loss of genuine enthusiasm (in the original sense of the term). Priests and ministers cling to their rituals out of fear or habit, and have nothing to teach the people but morality. The old Roman religion had grown as fossilized and uninspiring as modern 'Churchianity', yet the alternatives of agnosticism or atheism, while useful as a cleansing reaction, left the soul as bleak then as they do now. In answer to its need, illumination comes from another direction: *lux ex Oriente*. In those days it was the cults of Asia Minor, Egypt and the Near East that shed their light over the Empire; in these it is especially the discovery of the Far Eastern religions, in all their variety, which brings new life to the aspirations of those Westerners who are receptive to them. They proclaim that the sole purpose of life is spiritual development, for which each can find a means best suited in nature and level. Of course this could lead a modern person back to Christ, but then it would be with a new understanding and in a new relationship. Theory is transformed into experience, and mysteries – 'the hidden things' – become the central concern of life.

Too long have we learnt about ancient religion from unbelieving academics or from Christian chauvinists, divorcing it on the one hand from life and on the other from faith. I have the highest respect for the industry and dedication of our archaeologists and classicists, but not for the attitude that approaches the Mysteries in the same spirit as the classification of potsherds. Already the study of living religions is escaping from the obligatory agnosticism which used to be demanded by the modern Academy; and the case should be no different with ancient religion. I do not want to learn about Plato from a logical positivist, but from a Platonist. Is it possible to comprehend that in which one does not believe?

My frame of reference is the 'Perennial Philosophy', which I use for want of a better term to denote the philosophy that assumes a transcendent unity behind all religions, and sees them all as attempts, each valid for its time and place, to point the way to the true goal of human existence. Many people can accept this as it applies to the great religions current today: Hinduism, Buddhism, Christianity, Islam. But it is a different matter when it comes to religions as remote as those of Cybele, Mithras or Orpheus. Often they are regarded merely as bizarre and rather *fin-de-siècle* attempts to repair a loss of faith in the old Roman religion. They were much more than this. There were millions of devotees – human beings not so very different from ourselves – who lived and died in these – to us – strange faiths.

A deliberate effort of the imagination is necessary in order to comprehend them. It is not enough just to empathize with the religious impulse in general: one must put one's own self in the position, say, of a person for whom Cybele is God, and all that that can mean. In the case of a Mystery initiation, one must imagine one's entire life story, here and now, pivoting around the great event. Consider the high points of your life, the irrevocable stages and decisions that most affect your progress from birth to death: marriages, the choice of a career, meetings with remarkable persons . . . Imagine that there looms with comparable importance your initiation into the Mysteries of the Great Mother through the *taurobolium*, the ritual bull-sacrifice. Visualize yourself during the days of preparation: your nervousness, the expense and difficult stage-management of the event, culminating in that moment when you stand in the pit and are drenched in warm blood as the bull dies on the platform overhead. This is one of the things you have lived for, and you are never the same again.

I have chosen an extreme example – though not the most extreme, as readers will discover. Personally I find the idea repulsive, but much in the way that certain foods or diets may repel me. I do not for that reason call them poison. There are those who are nourished by them, and for whom they are absolutely right; and so I believe it is with religion. But how can one discover the rightness in practices and beliefs so far distanced from the modern appetite? Only through understanding that there are many ways to the goal, and many sorts and conditions of men, each treading his own path thither, whether he knows it or not.

The experiences and concerns of Mystery initiates are not the lot of all people, and are often inaccessible even in imagination to those who do not share them. The more intense they are, the more private they tend to be: if aired in public they only run the risk of being misunderstood. This is why there are 'mystery' religions. Mysteries are things which are kept silent, in order to avoid useless arguments and misapprehensions – and, at certain times and places, simply to keep one's head. People in the mass are xenophobic and hate that which they do not understand. If you have found a pearl, you do not throw it to the pigs, 'lest they turn and rend you'.

Silence was maintained with such admirable strictness in antiquity that the inquisitive researcher can discover very little of what went on in the rituals of these religions. The only things that were committed to writing were those which might be generally published; of the rest, memory was the best vault and silence the best guardian. But the most eloquent language of the Mysteries is not verbal but symbolic. Symbols elude the limiting precision of words, a precision which pins the ideas like butterflies to a single plane, while they should be free to flutter up and down all the levels of being and of meaning. It follows that in this book many of the visual images are susceptible to a multitude of interpretations, of which only one is suggested in the caption. The continual shifting of levels and of perspectives, which may at first seem capricious, is a deliberate exercise in expanding the mental response to symbolism.

The plates divide the subject according to the different religions, sects or cults, as they are usually studied by scholars. If one surveys them from a broader viewpoint, certain basic spiritual attitudes or orientations emerge, and these are described in the sections on the five Paths below. These five Paths are not peculiar to the period in question – they would mean little if they were. One or more of them is to be found in every human aspiration, no matter of what epoch or race. It is because they lead their followers along these archetypal paths that the Mystery religions are both justifiable and comprehensible.

The Path of the Warrior

Soldiering is not at present a reality to most people in the English-speaking world, especially those of the younger generation who have been spared the direct experience of warfare in their lifetimes. War for us, at the time of writing at least, is something that happens in the Third World. The ever-present threat of nuclear destruction under which we live is the very antithesis of hand-to-hand fighting with sharp weapons such as the ancients knew. Ancient societies, on the other hand, were intimate with war. Greek and Roman civilization had always been conducted on the assumption that this was part of life, as much as seed-time and harvest. War happened in between the two: while the crops were growing one went on campaign into the surrounding countryside, and fought with one's neighbours. Some men never returned, and that was as much to be expected as natural death. Others came home with booty and slaves, and that was good. War is always good for somebody, and bad for somebody else. So the soldier's outlook is always a dualistic one, or if you insist a selfish one. His whole object is to vanquish the opposition; and for this to be any sort of life for a man he has to have some belief in the validity and worth of his own cause. Even a motive so ignoble as racial superiority will serve: the soldier may feel perfectly justified in exterminating or enslaving a race or group he considers inferior for cultural or moral reasons, just as a gardener plucks out weeds so that more useful or beautiful plants may flourish in the same soil. No doubt the Germanic tribes and the Roman legionaries each felt this way about the other.

Belief in a cause is very easily transposed from a pragmatic to an idealistic level, and it does not take long for abstract concepts like Justice, Truth and Righteousness to be appropriated to one's own side. Given the trend in the ancient world towards personification, the virtues take on the personae of gods and goddesses, and instantly the hosts of heaven are enlisted to one's cause. Athena supported the Greeks as Hera did the Trojans, and the great Zeus himself was not indifferent to the outcome of a battle between mortals. The Dioscuri were glimpsed fighting alongside the Roman troops at Lake Regillus in *c.* 496 BC, just as the Angels of Mons appeared to the Allies in 1914. Prayers and sacrifices are offered up to ensure divine co-operation, for

1 *The Emperor Commodus as Hercules.* Statue, *c.* AD 192. Rome, Capitoline Museum.

'if God be for us, who can be against us?' The Crusaders set off with a high Mass to fight the enemies of Christ, while the Moslems trust in Allah to give them victory over the idolaters and polytheists. If war were not such a cruel business, one would have to laugh. But that were to take a God's-eye view. Let us consider rather what warfare, holy and otherwise, means to the individual soldier, and how it may actually constitute a valid spiritual path.

A soldier is called upon to hazard his bodily safety in the interests of a superior cause: for his country, his loved ones, his faith or his king. That means that he must place a higher value on these than on his person. He must also obey orders, submitting his own will to that of his officers. He accepts a life far removed from the comforts of home and family, and even though he hopes to return to them the richer for his exploits, he knows he may die and never see them again, or return maimed. All of this amounts to a powerful lesson in self-abasement. However arrogant the soldier may be on the surface, he surrenders his own individuality as soon as he dons his uniform and faces on the battlefield the possibility of his own annihilation. He comes very close to the mystery of death, and even if he appears none the wiser for it, it is a lesson for his soul that may bear fruit in time to come.

Some people are destined to live their whole lives within this context, and they are the world's warrior-caste whose job it is to rule and protect the people. Their calling is utterly different from that of the other traditional castes – priests and teachers, merchants and peasants – and different ethics apply to them as a result. When faced with the choice of killing or being killed, the perfect ascetic would give up his life; but the warrior should hit his adversary first! Most of the world's religions have made room for this attitude. The Japanese Samurai, the holy warriors Mohammed and Arjuna, the Knights of the Round Table: all are followers of this path.

In the case of Christianity there is an obvious disparity between Jesus's own pacifism and the behaviour of his followers. For some time before Jesus, the Essene brotherhood had followed ethical principles of the most rigorous kind, and if Jesus was, as seems likely, raised and educated by them, it is no surprise that his attitudes reflect their non-resistant ethics. Had these ethics continued to be the only acceptable ones for Church members, however, then Christianity would have remained, like the Essenes, an idiosyncratic Judaic sect. It would have had nothing to offer those whose nature and disposition prevents them from embracing this particular morality. Jesus had to be Lord of the warriors, the merchants and the peasants as well as of the ascetics. 'Gentle Jesus, meek and mild' therefore became, as

ii *Mithras slaying the Bull.* Statue from Rome, early second century A D. London, British Museum.

Christianity developed, also the terrible Judge of the World and General of the Church Militant, protecting his own flock like a Good Shepherd but disposing of his enemies with a soldier's forthrightness in the holocaust of Hell. Every Christian soldier could then identify with Jesus as Lord of the Last Judgment, and feel that he was doing his part in destroying the adversaries of his God – even if they also called themselves Christians.

Christianity was not the only cult thus to broaden its original base. The religion of Isis, which appealed in Imperial times largely to city-dwellers and middle-class women, welcomed Lucius (in Apuleius, *Metamorphoses* xi, 15) with the words: 'Enrol yourself in this holy military service.' But the allegiance of the actual warriors was more usually to the overtly military gods: Mars, Hercules, Sol Invictus, Jupiter Dolichenus, and especially Mithras. Mithraism was based on a real warrior's world-view. It imagined a supreme Lord of Light, powerful beyond any cosmos known to man, constantly opposed by the supreme Dark Lord Ahriman. Thus to the Mithraist the whole universe is in a perpetual state of warfare between the ultimately good and the ultimately evil. Mithras is a lower god whom Ormuzd sent to lead the side of the good within our cosmos – hence the Zodiac which often surrounds him and his acts. All of life is a battle, continuing even after death as devils and angels vie for possession of our souls. So war between humans is only to be expected as an image of the cosmic and even metacosmic strife. Outwardly, a soldier of Mithras must ally his energies and aspirations with the side of the angels. Inwardly he must make his life a continuous re-enactment of the creative bull-sacrifice (see illustration), mortifying the merely physical, symbolized by the bull, so that the life-giving spirit may flow forth more abundantly.

The simile of a soldier rising from the ranks through successive promotions could aptly be applied to the series of initiatic grades which Mithraism and the other Mystery religions offered their devotees. The warrior would hope to develop in the course of initiations an increasing detachment from personal concerns and from fear, and a capacity to make reliable but rapid decisions on matters of life and death. As a modern 'warrior path' one could cite Freemasonry, always strong in the Armed Forces, with its typical stress on the military virtues of brotherhood and loyalty, its secret and sometimes daunting initiations, its system of degrees and the formidable political power which it has exercised behind the scenes of history. And as a path on the individual level, rather than the collective one, there is the complex of Martial Arts which have long been cultivated in the Far East. These take the necessities of a warrior's existence as the basis for developing spiritual qualities, especially that of acting at lightning speed on the strength of intuition rather than thought. Extrapolating from what is known of these modern phenomena, one may approach in imagination the ancient military cults.

Life on earth, according to the Perennial Philosophy, is like a school in which human souls are subjected to various tests, some of a more or less painful nature; and it is only through these experiences or initiations that progress can be made. Not only the conscious aspirant but every person alive or dead is engaged on the Herculean task of raising himself from the status of an animal to that of a god. Sometimes the tests, and the changes in consciousness which they demand, come quietly. Sometimes they occur purely on a mental level. But at other times, and especially when the person is in some way dense or insensitive, they will descend and take the form of physical accident or illness. Then a battle ensues between the forces of healing and those that seek to destroy the body. Exactly so in the collectivity: there are social and cultural changes that are inevitable 'initiations' of mankind. If they are accepted, they can take place peacefully and progress will be smooth. If they are resisted, they will come all the same, but will occur on a physical level as war or bloody revolution.

The period under scrutiny – the first four or five centuries A D – saw changes of both kinds. Perhaps the most far-reaching result was the extension throughout the Empire of the privilege of Roman citizenship, with all the encouragement this gave people to see themselves as individual members of a vast family, rather than as unconscious fragments of a tribe or provincial race. This step was achieved partly by peaceful acquiescence, partly by forcible conquest. Nowadays we are facing a similar prospect, only on a global scale, with the same options.

When change has to happen in a violent way, the instigator may be a kind of avatar or divine incarnation of a minor order, charged like a surgeon with the distasteful task of operating on the body politic. He may be chosen for his manipulative skill, as it were, rather than for any conscious understanding of the matter in hand. The Emperor Julian, for example, understood very well the profound spiritual currents of his age, and tried to reverse them without success: he was not a practical man. Alexander the Great, on the other hand (who with good reason was one of Julian's heroes), was supremely practical, yet confessed that he was not his own master. When questioned by the Indian Brahmins on why he persisted in waging war, he replied as follows:

It is ordained by heavenly Providence that we should be servants of the gods' decree. The sea does not rise in waves unless the wind blows, nor is the tree set in motion unless the wind touches it; so also man does not act unless he is impelled by the heavenly Providence. I would willingly desist from making war, but the Lord of my spirit does not suffer me to do so. For if all were of one mind, the cosmos would stand still . . . (Pseudo-Callisthenes 3, 6)

He might have been speaking for the human race as a whole.

iii *The Emperor as Cosmic Victor*. The 'Ludovisi' Sarcophagus of Hostilianus, AD 251. Rome, National Museum.

The Path of the Monk

The monk's path, like the warrior's, is based on a dualistic vision of the cosmos. The essential difference lies in this: while the warrior's enemy is without, the monk's lies within himself. Of course this does not prevent an ascetic (like the Ayatollah Khomeini) from seeing Satan incarnate in his fellow men, any more than it prevents a warrior (like T. E. Lawrence or the ideal Mithraist) from being a master of self-denial. All these 'paths' are extremes, and most people's aspirations lie along more than one of them.

Fundamental to the monk's attitude is a duality of spirit and matter, which is manifested in the human being as a gulf between soul and body. It is the ascetic's view that the spirit or soul has become entangled in the material world, or in the human body, and that it is the purpose of religion to free it. For the Orphics and Pythagoreans, our existence on earth is forced upon us as expiation of our sins. It is a terrible thing for one's soul to be imprisoned in the physical body: no wonder new-born babies cry. When the disciples of the great Indian sage, Ramana Maharshi, wanted to celebrate his birthday, the master said: 'On one's birthday one should mourn one's entry into this world' (*Collected Works*, p. 137).

For all the philosophers of the Pythagorean-Platonic-Hermetic tradition, the situation is the same. The universe is a hierarchy of different states of being, of which the very lowest is our tangible world and the things made of its four elements: earth, water, air and fire. Everything in this region, the sphere beneath the Moon, is imperfect and subject to pain, suffering, decay and death. Beyond, in the ethereal spheres of the planets, we would find progressively purer states, and above the fixed stars is the realm of the gods where perfection reigns – at least from our point of view. The higher or Rational Soul in man belongs to that realm and knows it as its home; but here on earth it is stifled, sunk in the intractable clay of our physical frame. The ascetic's task is to release it, and he does this by wearing away, by one means or another, the prison of flesh and blood.

iv *Hor, a Priest of Thoth.* Basalt statue from Alexandria, early first century AD (?) Cairo, National Museum.

Profane people mistakenly love their bodies, ignorant of the divine spark that lies captive therein. They delight in pampering their bodies with food and drink, and in clothing them with cosmetics and raiment. They take pride in that of which they ought to be most ashamed. Thus the monk thinks as he watches worldly folk. He, on the other hand, has made a commitment to release himself from these vanities. His road is asceticism, and it differs little whether he be an Egyptian priest (see illustration, p. 16), a Christian nun or monk, a Jewish Essene or a member of the Pythagorean brotherhood.

Ascesis consists in the relinquishing of one pleasure in the hope of gaining a greater one. The weight-watcher renounces certain foods for the greater delight of being slim. The vegetarian does so for the higher ideal of humanitarianism. And the monk fasts for the joy of release from bondage to the stomach's demands – and, no doubt, for the pleasant 'high' that prolonged abstinence brings. Fasting strengthens the will and purifies the body. Like all asceticisms, it may be taken to extremes. The medieval Cathars of Montaillou, when they felt death approaching, would sometimes start the *endura*, the fast unto death, refusing all nourishment. To maintain such a vow to the end was a highly respected achievement, and deemed a great benefit to the soul. In the more sophisticated environment of the ancient Essenes, a similar practice was usual among the very old who no longer desired life. After bidding farewell to the community they would go alone into a deserted place where there was water, carrying with them a bunch of grapes. Each day they would eat a few grapes, and when those were gone they would drink only water, spending their time in spiritual exercises until a peaceful death supervened. What a contrast to the struggles of modern medicine to keep us alive at any price!

The Essenes and the Pythagoreans were supposed to be vegetarians, though in the case of the latter it is doubtful that all schools followed the master's example. Apart from the obvious motive of compassion towards one's fellow creatures, vegetarianism has also the purpose of purifying the body from the contaminations of flesh foods. Purification, however, could incur dietary rules of a quite different sort. The Neoplatonic Emperor Julian was not a vegetarian, but he refrained from root vegetables because they bring into the body a downward tendency [Rudolf Steiner would have said the opposite]; from apples for they are too holy; from the pomegranate because it belongs to the Underworld; from dates because they are too solar; from fish because they are not usually sacrificed to the gods, and anyway come from too deep down; and from pigs because they are coarse, earthly, vile creatures, only offered to the chthonic gods (*Orations* v, 175–7).

The idea of contamination also extends to the company of other humans. Any sensitive person who does not habitually live in a large modern city knows what psychic contamination is, and feels it when in such a hive of humanity. The Desert Fathers put not only the temptations of the city but all human contact behind them as they went off to face themselves and their God. Their physical courage in a wilderness full of dangers was only exceeded by the mental and emotional stamina with which they encountered what they knew as demonic forces – no matter that we might call them projections from the darker realms of the psyche. St Anthony emerged from his ordeal 'as one initiated into sacred Mysteries', with knowledge of the unseen world and power over it (Athanasius, *Vita S. Antonii* 14). Such men did not need the formal initiations of the Mystery cults: they had passed the same gates on their own.

Many of the cults made use of mild asceticism for the benefit of those who were content to live, for the most part, a worldly life. Lucius had to abstain from meat, wine and sexual intercourse for the ten days preceding his initiation into the Mysteries of Osiris (*Metamorphoses* xi, 28), and Propertius complains that his Cynthia is observing a similar period of chastity in preparation for the rites of Isis (*Elegy* 33). Traditional Catholicism continued in this practice with the regular fasts throughout the Church's year, and restrictions on the timing and nature of sexual activity, while the making of retreats is a universal religious observance, giving the advantages of a temporary monasticism.

It is chastity above all that distinguishes the monk's life from that of lay people. If he considers birth a tragedy, then the logical response is to avoid causing the fall of other human souls into bodies. Some later Gnostics renounced reproduction altogether, as did the American Shakers in the nineteenth century – and quickly became extinct. But there is another, personal side to chastity. The power to reproduce one's kind is a marvellous and magical power, and it can be harnessed to other ends. Sexual energy, as the Indian yogis know, is one manifestation of that greater creative energy which can bring about a spiritual birth in higher worlds if it is not used up for pleasure and reproduction in this world. It is this knowledge, generalized and wrongly applied, that has given many un-ascetic religious people their sheepish attitude towards sex. St Paul tells the Corinthians (I: 7, 9) that 'it is better to marry than to burn' – better still not to need to marry. The sublimated urges of fanatical monks have been spent in tyranny of their fellows as often as they have lifted them above earthly desires.

The belief that sex is a hindrance to spiritual achievement, taken naïvely, led in ancient times to the grotesque extreme of voluntary castration. The enlightened Christian Father Origen tried this in his youth in the hope of escaping from his desires, and lived to see that it was not the way: indeed, it is specifically forbidden to Christians. Not so to the followers of Cybele and Attis, whose eunuch priests, the Galli, were the most notorious practitioners of this parody of continence (see illustration). Perhaps today's 'transexuals' are reincarnations of these fanatics, who after their castration would adopt feminine costume and extravagant adornments. The Emperor Domitian in the first century A D made castration a capital crime, but did not succeed in preventing the practice any more than Hadrian, who tried to prohibit circumcision: a symbolic substitute used by ancient Egyptians and Arabs as well as Jews. The Emperor Elagabalus, keen to embrace every cult, is said to have circumcised himself and refrained from eating pork; he further planned to honour the Great Mother by having himself castrated, but either did not live long enough, or changed his mind when he decided to violate a Vestal Virgin. Some of his followers went to the uttermost extreme of renunciation in hurling their most beautiful children to the wild beasts in his temple.

It is sometimes difficult, in the world of ascetics, to distinguish sober purification from wilful self-punishment. Juvenal mocks the women devotees of Isis who stand in the icy Tiber or crawl on bleeding knees to her temple (*Satire* 6, 522–6). Herodotus, at the Isis festival in Busiris, witnessed myriads of people in orgiastic flagellation (*History* ii, 61). The Gallus in the plate holds a fierce-looking whip in his left hand. The theme of mortification of the flesh runs throughout Christian monasticism: from St Jerome in the desert, beating his breast with a stone, through Savonarola's hair-shirt, to the little scourges issued to modern nuns. And were not the tortures of the Inquisition a forced asceticism, a monstrous perversion of the theme that the body must suffer if the soul is to go free?

v *A 'Gallus', Eunuch Priest of the Great Mother*. Relief from the Appian Way, mid-second century A D. Rome, Capitoline Museum.

X · DONO · DVCIS · SFORTIAE · SFORTIAE

The Path of the Magician

The magician's attitude to the gulf between body and spirit is to unite them. A believer, like the monk, in a hierarchical universe of which our earth is the lowest level, he does not try to abandon or deny the physical world and body: he uses them. Mindful of the axiom of Hermes Trismegistus, patron of magical arts: 'Whatever is above is like to that below: and whatever is below is like to that above', he respects the correspondences and similarities between all levels of the universe. He knows that man is a microcosm, and that even his physical frame is made, in some sense, in God's image. All the levels of existence mirror one another in structure. When the structures are set in motion, a similar movement is felt throughout the hierarchy.

The most obvious example of this world-view is astrology, which assumes that the movements of the planets are reflected in world events and in the human psyche. A fatalistic believer in astrology resigns himself to an ineluctable destiny, deeming himself no more capable of opposition to the planets than the magnetic needle is able to point away from the North Pole. But the magician, by contrast, exploits the system of correspondences, knowing that their 'causality', if such it be, works in both directions. Whatever is done on earth is mirrored in the heavens: and who can say which is cause, and which effect? Magic is the science of affecting the unseen worlds through operations conducted on this one.

The commonest form of magic practised in the ancient world was animal sacrifice. Regarded from the point of view of a simple-minded worshipper, the victim's life-force is offered as a kind of food to the god. (Usually the body would be divided between donor and clergy, and eaten: complete incineration was exceptional.) Such a gift incurred an obligation on the god's part, or at least encouraged reciprocal favours. As Porphyry categorizes it, sacrifice can be made for three purposes: homage, necessity or gratitude, and none are really disinterested. Regarded esoterically, however, the picture is a little different. Animal sacrifice affects not the true gods, but the sublunary elementals: invisible spirits who throng the earth's atmosphere and live on matter of an etheric kind. They may, under

certain circumstances, render services to men, but they are tricky characters, at best indifferent to humans, and not to be relied upon. Hence Christians shunned them, and refused any part in the animal slaughter which attracts them. Constantine offered God only flowers and incense, and Theodosius, in his edicts of AD 391, made sacrifice illegal throughout the Empire. Some contemporary pagan philosophers, notably Porphyry (*De Abstinentia* ii, 12), also renounced animal killing, thinking that it cannot possibly affect the gods, that its consequences are not favourable to humans.

A special case of sacrifice, and one that belongs to another category of magic, was the *taurobolium*, already mentioned above. In this ritual bull-slaughter, the vital forces of the bull are poured out with the blood over the devotee. Extraordinary power was attributed to this act, and those who had undergone the experience were celebrated as 'eternally reborn'. The taurobolium began as an ordinary bull-sacrifice, common in the ancient world (cf. Homer's 'hecatombs of

vi *Triple Hecate*. Miniature bronze altar for use in sympathetic magic. From Pergamum, AD 200–50. Berlin, Staatliche Museen.

23

vii *Phallic Tintinnabulum.* Bronze from Pompeii, *c.* first century AD. London, British Museum.

oxen'), but took on a more religious slant in the second century AD when the bull's blood was distributed in a kind of communion to the faithful. At the same time the genitals were removed and specially buried: and this connects with the rites of the Great Mother Cybele, recalling and perhaps re-enacting the castration of Attis (see Chapter X). The full ritual, established *c.* AD 300, was intended to transmute the physical strength of the bull into psychic energy for the benefit of the participant or for another assigned by him. Here are two of the fundamental aspects of later magic: the harnessing of the energy inherent in blood, and of sexual energy, for defensive, offensive or sublimatory purposes. The phallic form of many ancient charms (see illustration) is similarly a means of bringing the creative and essentially positive power of Nature to aid against the entropic and destructive designs of 'evil' forces.

The last taurobolium in Rome was celebrated in the late fourth century AD, on the site now occupied by St Peter's. But ritual bull-sacrifice was a regular practice in the more remote areas of Thrace, in northern Greece, well on into the twentieth century. Kakouri (see Bibliography) tells of the nominally Christian body of initiates who, under the patronage of Saints Helena and Constantine still preside there over fire-walking and phallic fertility dramas. In their bull-sacrifice, the unblemished victim had to come of his own free will, and after the slaughter his flesh was partly consumed raw. In a poor society such as existed in Thrace and much of the ancient world, most of the meat ever eaten must have been butchered at sacrifices: Homer's heroes only enjoy it on such occasions. The modern person who reacts with distaste to the idea of animal sacrifice might reflect on the dignity and respect paid to the victim, and to the spiritual intentions surrounding the ceremony, in contrast to the degrading and godless slaughtering practised today.

Some pagans defended sacrifice, while recognizing that it cannot possibly affect the eternal gods. Sallust admitted that they gain nothing from it, but that we gain everything (*On the Gods* 15). Julian encouraged it in his pagan revival, along with the reverence of statues of the gods, as conducive to piety, considering the subjective state of the worshipper to be its justification. One should be eager to offer up one's best to the gods, he said, just as one should delight in seeing their images (*Against the Galilaeans* 347C; *Letters* 293C–D). But representations of the gods are not mere reminders: like the relics of saints and heroes, they have as their purpose the drawing down of celestial influences. The magical charm shown here (see illustration) was worn for protection against the Evil Eye, just like the blue glass charms and medals of saints sold around the Mediterranean today. And the Hecate plaque (see illustration, p. 23) served like a modern radionic device to direct invisible influences on to whatever was placed on the little table in the middle – perhaps a lock of hair, or fingernail, as in witchcraft. The magic used here was probably 'grey', if not actually black.

To distinguish white magic from black, one must ask whether it is the intention of the magical act to elevate the lower towards a higher plane or goal, or else to exploit the higher forces in order to obtain advantages on the lower level. Apuleius started out meddling with the inferior sort, and got into trouble which he describes in his *Apology*, but then rose to the higher magic of theurgy. A theurgist is a magician who seeks through his knowledge to align earthly things with the divine order, so that 'Thy will be done on earth, as it is in heaven.' But he cannot join two things so far apart without an intermediary. The late antique theurgists did not believe that they were actually contacting, much less commanding, the gods themselves. They knew that they were dealing with the good daemons who fill the links in the chain of being between gods and men. These daemons partake of the characteristics of the gods to which they themselves are devoted, and hence serve as channels for the different divine forces to descend to earth. They like to be addressed by the names of their archetypal divinities, and they respond only to absolutely correct procedures. As Iamblichus says, to get the slightest detail of an incantation or ceremony wrong can invalidate the entire operation. One might as well try to give a concert with one lyre-string broken (*De Mysteriis* v, 21). The same situation is well known today in the form of 'natural magic' which we prefer to call experimental science.

The Christian magical rites – the seven sacraments – are essentially acts of theurgy, in which something on the physical plane (bread, oil, a ring, etc.) is manipulated with certain spoken formulae in order to make changes occur on an invisible or 'subtle' plane. Clairvoyants say that changes happen there with an ease and a rapidity denied to physical matter. What is affected is primarily the subtle bodies of the participants, with the object in view being ideally not material gain but perfection. Through the subtly transmuted elements of water, bread and wine, the Christian sacraments of Baptism and the Eucharist are believed to draw down the forces of Christ into the souls of the participants. This direct contact with the god is something foreign to the magician, but nothing less is attempted by those on the more direct Path of Love.

viii *Talisman against the Evil Eye*. (*top*) 'Solomon' kills a she-devil. (*above*) Four beasts attack the Eye. Bronze pendant, before AD 325. University of Pennsylvania Museum.

The Path of Love

Just as the magician sees all the levels of the universe linked by a chain of correspondences, the person of the Path of Love sees them joined by mutual affection. According to his world-view, God so loves the world that he or she sends the divine influences down into its very depths, cherishing every creature with a more than motherly love (see illustration). Conversely, man can so love God that he is raised to divine union. The ultimate object is 'nothing else than existing in God himself' (St Gregory of Nyssa). Like all human beings, the devotee starts out on his path sundered from his object of adoration, and his lifelong aspiration is towards closing the gap. In the end the lover is no longer distinct from the beloved, the two are become one, and the difference in levels is transcended. This is fully as miraculous as the magical joining of heaven and earth: even more so, since the magician has the benefit of a scientific system, while the lover works only with the power within his own soul. He is nothing, God is everything, as he seeks the absorption of the part into the whole, of the human fragment into the One. A Hermetic fragment puts the idea of union very vividly: 'Come into me, Hermes, as children come into women's wombs. I know thee, Hermes, and thou knowest me: I am thou, and thou art I . . .' (Kenyon, *Greek Papyri*, I, p. 116).

But these are the higher flights of advanced mystics who have no need for an anthropomorphic intermediary between themselves and the Divine. Most devotees address an image of the god, made with hands or the inner eye, and conceive him or her as having at least some human traits: hence the many saviours and heroes described in these pages. Unlike the gods of Olympus, the Mystery gods have usually suffered pain, loss or death, and this gives them compassion for our own sufferings and joys. Osiris, Orpheus, Hercules, Christ, Dionysus, Attis and Adonis were all slain and resurrected. But of all the gods of the Mystery religions, perhaps the best-loved was Isis – loved for her warm humanity and for incarnating all the best aspects of woman as lover, wife, mother and widow. Apuleius or his fictional character Lucius, on renouncing his debauched past, recognizes the true consummation of *eros* in mystic union with her, and devotes himself

ix *Isis nursing Horus.* Terracotta from Herculaneum, *c.* first century A.D. Naples, National Museum.

x *Dionysian Revelry*. Painting from the Tomb of the Nasonii, Rome, later third century A D. London, British Museum.

to her service much as a medieval knight would swear fealty to the Virgin Mary. In her epiphany to him, she assures him that she is everything and everywhere: 'You will worship me even in Hades' (*Metamorphoses* xi, 6). All the Mystery gods descended to the underworld, too, to redeem those incarcerated there. The same idea occurs in the Buddhist system, where every world, even Hell, contains a Boddhisattva. Nowhere in the universe is love absent from him who truly opens himself to it.

Isis was an indulgent mistress, imposing no particular morality beyond the natural inclinations of good men. 'Love, and do what thou wilt' might have been her motto, for love will turn all to good. But those on the Path of Love often become acutely aware of the impurity and unworthiness of the human state, and are hence drawn also to the path of purification and ascesis. They then manifest a blend of self-denial and adoration such as was later to become so characteristic of Christian saints.

If one had to single out one paramount feature that distinguished all the Mystery cults from other religions of their period, it would be that they sought a personal relationship with their gods. Consequently the attitude of their devotees to the gods was one of love rather than of fear or indifferent manipulation. The motive of much primitive religion seems to be to get rid of the gods, and by fair means or foul to prevent them from troubling mankind. For the Mystery religions the motive is quite the contrary: it is to get closer to them, recognizing them as man's best friends. The Maenads of Dionysus (see illustration) are more than that even: the god is their lover. One of the tasks of Christ was to open this path of direct intimacy with God to

27

every person without distinction, cutting through the barriers of race and class like many of the cults contemporary with him.

The path of loving devotion to the gods does not necessarily call for any external ceremonies or human intermediaries, but in actual practice it is usually combined with one or more of the other paths, and rituals and initiations are used to further the progress of the aspirant. One such means, not in any way peculiar to Christianity, is holy communion, in which the goal of assimilation to the god on his level is furthered by assimilation of him on this plane. Dionysus was believed to be present, not merely symbolically but actually, in the wine and raw flesh which his devotees consumed. A Persian Mithraic text, amazingly reminiscent of Jesus's words, states that 'he who will not eat of my body and drink of my blood, so that he will be made one with me and I with him, the same shall not know salvation.' The initiates of Cybele and Attis had some form of communion, too, for they declared: 'I have eaten from the tambourine: I have drunk from the cymbal' – the instruments sacred to them – but what they ate or drank we do not know.

Another aspect of communion is that as a sacred meal it prefigures the celestial banquet which the blessed are thought to enjoy in heaven, in the eternal presence of Christ, Serapis, Mithras, or other banqueting saviours. Some of the Mysteries went further to anticipate the ambience of heaven by inducing unworldly states. Wine probably affected the ancients far more powerfully than it does us (they seldom drank it unmixed with water), but even the sober Plato allows intoxication at the Dionysian festivals (*Laws* 775B): 'Rather the madness of the god than the sobriety of men' (*Phaedrus* 244D). In the Mysteries, all five senses might be elevated through wine, music, lights, incense and sexuality, to say nothing of drugs, in order to create an unforgettable experience and encourage hopes of heavenly bliss. According to the Platonic view, the things and people that we love on earth are sent us for the same reason: we love them because they remind our souls of the paradise from which we came, and to which we may eventually return. The Neoplatonists applied this doctrine to mythology in order to justify the love-life of the gods. The abduction of the Leuccipid women by the Dioscuri (see illustration), for example, denotes the seizure of the soul by the irresistible forces of divine love, after which its sole joy is to live in the house of the Lord for ever.

When Christ urged his followers to 'hate' their human relations before they could become his disciples (Luke 14, 26), he was likewise demanding that they transfer their earthly affections to a divine

xi *Abduction of a Leucippid.* Stucco decoration, first century AD. Rome, Porta Maggiore Basilica.

xii *Christ preaching the Sermon on the Mount*. Sarcophagus from Vigna Maccarani, *c*.AD 270–310. Rome, National Museum.

object. Far from inducing hatred, this only serves to make a person more loving in his transactions with mankind, for he now shares in the reciprocal action of the gods' love for all men. So Christ in his Sermon on the Mount (see illustration) could equally well say, 'Love your enemies' (Matthew 5, 44). Nearly all religions admit that there are beings in the universe who have reached a stage of spiritual evolution inconceivable to us, some of whom make it their work to help lower creatures such as mankind. The Christ was one; the Bodhisattvas of Buddhism and the Avatars of the Hindus are others. Out of compassion and truly divine love they may descend to this and other earths and take on the burden of a human body. For such beings, physical incarnation is a veritable crucifixion: a nailing of their divinity to the fourfold cross of the elements. This is the esoteric meaning of Christ's love for us, and of his symbolic death on the cross.

The Path of Knowledge

When the goal of love is consummated, what is left? Perfect knowledge that is at once possession and being. You are what you know. Knowledge, even on a mundane level, involves the actual taking of the object into oneself. On a mystical level this process is felt as the dissolution of difference between subject and object: the two become one single self-knowing act. The person on the Path of Love experiences this with an emotional colouring – which in turn is part of the knowledge. Ultimately, all paths bring knowledge to those who tread them: whatever their effect in the world outside, their inner purpose is to bring man closer to the knowledge of God. The warrior and the monk, each in his way, allies himself with the side of what he sees as the Divine, rejecting all else, that he may more closely know that to which he belongs. The magician strives to know God's mind as it is exteriorized in the cosmic patterns. Philo says that man reaches out to God through mediators: the Logos and Angelic Powers – but that ultimately man is allied to God himself through his Intellect. He means by this term not the logical mind, but the 'Rational Soul' of the Platonists, the Hindus' *Buddhi*: a fragment of the divine nature itself which enables man to rise in his higher understanding to the very throne of God. 'When the soul that loves God searches into the nature of the Existent, it enters into a search for the formless and the invisible. The greatest thing it understands from this is the comprehension that God is incomprehensible and the vision that he is invisible' (*De Posteritate Caini* 15).

The knowledge gained by those enlightened beings who have risen so far is not expressible in human language. But there are lower stages on the Path of Knowledge which are a preparation for the ultimate experiences. Plutarch says that

A desire for the truth, especially about the gods, is in reality a yearning for the Deity. For the study and the search is a reception, as it were, of things sacred – an occupation more pious than any practice of abstinence or service in a temple, but particularly well pleasing to this goddess [Isis] whom you worship, for she is both exceedingly wise and a lover of wisdom. (*De Iside et Osiride* 2)

xiii *The Philosopher Plotinus.* Supposed portrait from Ostia, *c.* AD 260. Ostia, Museo Ostiense.

Plutarch's near contemporary Philo Judaeus describes from his own experience how wisdom of a higher order can unexpectedly descend on the student:

Sometimes I have approached my work empty, and suddenly become full, the ideas falling in a shower from above and being sown invisibly, so that under the influence of the Divine possession I have been filled with corybantic fury and been unconscious of anything: place, persons, myself, words spoken, lines written. For I obtained language, ideas, an enjoyment of light, keenest vision, pellucid distinction of objects, such as might be reached through the eyes as the result of hypernormal clarity. (*De Migratione Abrahami* 35)

The Path of Knowledge is through study and meditation. What is studied is for the most part the findings of those who have progressed further than the student. In the ancient world this path was followed primarily by those in philosophical schools such as Plato's Academy in Athens (which was not closed until AD 529), the circle of Plotinus (see illustration, p. 30) in Rome, and the Alexandrian Neo-pythagorean, Neoplatonic and Gnostic schools. Unlike the Peripatetics, Stoics and Epicureans, these students accepted the existence of revealed doctrines and revered certain of their masters as recipients of a higher learning inaccessible to the logical mind. Philo speaks of how the spirit of a Prophet can be replaced, temporarily or permanently, by the Divine Spirit. Plutarch, writing on the nature of Socrates' inspiration, explained that his daemon was, unlike ours, a pure one, able to hear the divine message. The daemon of Plotinus was similarly said to be an entity of the order of gods, giving him direct access to higher knowledge. St Gregory sensed in Origen the voice not of a human being but of the 'Angel of the Great Counsel'. And the Pythagoreans believed their master to be an incarnation of Apollo. Early Christian art, shunning altogether the subject of the Crucifixion, often shows Jesus as the teacher of his disciples, passing on the Word of God (see illustration), reminding us of the Gnostic tradition that there was a secret dimension to his teachings which was reserved for the closer disciples, and thus assimilating Jesus to the tradition of inspired philosophical teachers.

In antiquity there was another avenue to divine knowledge open to the earnest aspirant, and that was the Mysteries themselves. In Greece there had been an initiatic institution at Eleusis at least since the eighth century BC, with both Greater and Lesser Mysteries. It is gratifying to reflect that modern scholars still do not know what went on in these ceremonies, so well was secrecy maintained for over a thousand years of annual celebration. According to occultists, the function of all

Lesser Mysteries, or equally of the lower grades of initiation, was to impart information on the nature of higher worlds, while that of Greater Mysteries was to bring about direct contact with the beings who inhabit them. Some scholars imagine the Mysteries of Eleusis and other institutions to have been merely a sacred drama played by actors to fill an impressionable audience with holy dread. Yet the architecture of the great hall at Eleusis, the Telesterion, certainly precludes this: the room was filled with pillars. On the other hand, the great number of lesser initiates there ruled out individual treatment. Something can only have happened on the psychic plane which touched every person present: a collective vision which left an unforgettable impression. The Eleusinian symbolism of corn, pomegranates and poppies (see illustration p. 34) refers to the unseen forces which affect mankind via the vegetable kingdom, building the body and informing the mind. The intuitive grasp of this relationship, in all its wonder and complexity, was summarized in the famous climax of

xiv *Christ as a Philosophical Teacher*. Ivory plaque, fourth century AD. Brescia, Museo Civico.

xv *The Poppy as Mediator between Earth and Heaven*. Vase from Apulia, fourth century BC. Vatican Museum.

the Mystery, so disappointing to non-initiates: the displaying of an ear of wheat. Certain information was also given at Eleusis by word of mouth, including the 'password to the Paradise of Demeter' to be used after death. In the Lesser Mysteries of other gods, it is suggested that the fact of heliocentricity was revealed. Jewish esotericism includes the teaching of reincarnation. So Lesser Mysteries give the initiates theoretical knowledge which changes their whole view of man and the cosmos, and stands them in better stead when they have to leave this world for the unknown. Nowadays this information is available freely, and each person can decide whether or not to make the change from accepted attitudes which constitutes the first initiation.

The Greater Mysteries, or higher grades of initiation, were conducted individually rather than collectively. The initiations of Isis were given to those priests or laity selected by the goddess through having had significant dreams. Sometimes the dream itself might be the initiation: the late Platonist Damascius dreamed: 'I had become Attis and the Great Mother was celebrating the Hilaria [feast of Cybele] in my honour' (*Vita Isidori* 131). From this he acquired the certitude of eternal salvation.

But the primary object of these initiations was to take the candidate through the gates of death. The hierophant told Apuleius before his initiation that it was like a voluntary death followed by a slow recovery. Plutarch, conversely, said that when death comes it is like initiation into the Greater Mysteries (see quotation below). As in shamanic, Masonic, and other later initiations, the candidate was placed in a trance, his consciousness taken out of his body, and in this state he experienced higher states of being and met some of the denizens of the invisible worlds. Some were demonic, others beneficent; Proclus describes certain of them as forms of light that take on human shape (*In Rempublicam* i, 110–11). Through direct experience the candidate would learn that he could live freely without his physical body, and that the gods he worshipped were perfectly real. Then he would return to earth fully convinced of his immortality and prepared to meet death fearlessly, knowing it as the gate to freedom and his soul's true home.

Since earthly life is so short and its limitations so unsatisfactory, it is not surprising that the Mystery religions were largely concerned with what happens afterwards. They sought to give foreknowledge of the posthumous state, in order to save souls from the confusion they would otherwise face on entering the immaterial world. Like the Egyptian and Oriental 'Books of the Dead', they gave instructions for the journey. Our ideas of this journey are of necessity compiled from a large number of fragmentary accounts, some of them seemingly contradictory. This is because the subjective experience of the journey will be different for every person, just as life on earth is differently experienced by everyone. Yet certain features are common to all men. Using the terms of exoteric religion, some Mystery texts describe the soul as first going to Hades, but this underworld is clearly no longer a dark place beneath the earth's surface, as it was in traditional religion (see Cumont in *CRAI*, 1920, p. 272). The underworld over which Serapis rules is the lowest of the heavens, i.e. the sphere beneath the Moon. At the gate of Hades, the soul is said to meet its earthly master; alternatively, it may meet a celestial psychopomp such as Hermes, Jesus, Mithras or Anubis, who acts as its guide and guardian. Some form of judgment follows, after which, in abbreviated accounts, the soul proceeds to its appointed place: good souls to blissful union with the gods, bad ones to punishments and both, perhaps, to eventual rebirth on the earth.

In more elaborate accounts of the soul's voyage, it ascends first through the airy regions where it is purified by the action of the winds (*Aeneid* vi, 740–6). The wind gods, sometimes identified with the Seasons, 'winnow' the soul, refining it until it is fit to continue on its way into more ethereal climes. (This is the significance of the winnowing-basket in Dionysian symbolism.) Plutarch calls this region the Meadows of Hades – evidently the same as the Elysian Fields whence Orpheus fetched Eurydice – and says that the sojourn therein is shorter for the more temperate souls who are less in need of purification (*On the Face in the Moon* 945). An Orphic sect active from the sixth to the second centuries BC buried with its dead gold leaves, on one of which was inscribed the following beautiful description of what to expect in these meadows:

You will find in the well-built dwellings of Hades, on the right, a spring near a white cypress. The souls of the dead go down there seeking refreshment; but do not on any account approach it. You will find another whose chill waters flow from the Lake of Mnemosyne. Before it stand guardians, who will ask you why you come, searching the darkness of Hades. Say to them: 'I am a child of the earth and the starry heaven; I am dried up from thirst and I perish; but give me quickly the cold water which flows from the Lake of Memory.' And being servants of the King of the Underworld, they will have compassion on you and give you to drink of the Lake. And then you can follow on the sacred way the glorious procession of the other *Mystai* and *Bacchoi*. (Guarducci, *Epigrafia Greca*, IV, p. 263)

In a fragment preserved by Stobaeus, Plutarch gives an encapsulated description of the soul's experiences so far:

Thus death and initiation closely correspond. At first there are wanderings and toilsome running about in circles, and journeys through the dark over uncertain roads and dead ends; then, just before the end, there are all kinds of terrors, with shivering, trembling, sweating and utter amazement. After this, a strange and wonderful light meets the wanderer; he is admitted into pure and verdant pastures, where he discerns gentle voices, solemn dances, and the majesty of blessed spirits and sacred visions. Here he is free, being now fully initiated, and walks at liberty like a crowned and dedicated sacrificial victim, joining in the revelry. (*Fragment* 178, Loeb edition)

For many, this is the end of the journey as they envisage it. But above Hades lie the seven planetary spheres, which must eventually be crossed. These are experienced as obstacles or gates, and the Mystery religions offered special knowledge to assist the soul in passing each one: passwords, formulae, seals. The Mithraists, true to their Manichaean cosmos, imagined that good and evil daemons fight there for possession of souls – an idea not unknown to Christianity. For others the battle is more within the soul itself, for in order to pass each level it has to divest itself of the energies or tendencies ruled by that planet. At the Moon it leaves behind the power of growth, at Mars the irascible impulses, etc. (see Macrobius, *In Somnium Scipionis*

i, 12). By the time it attains the heaven of the fixed stars, it is entirely free from all its lower qualities, and escapes from the circles of the cosmos to live with the gods in their realm of perfection. As a Dionysian inscription says, 'I have flown out of the sorrowful, weary wheel; I have pursued with eager feet to the circle desired' (Kaibel, *Inscriptiones*, no. 641).

It is this realm, and the way there, that are shown in the frescoes of the Villa of the Mysteries at Pompeii (see illustration), where humans mix freely with sub- and superhuman beings. The Orphics called this sphere of the visible universe the Circle of Necessity; Buddhists call it the Wheel of Existence. According to both, the soul can take two alternative routes when it leaves the body: it can either remain within the Wheel, in which case it will sooner or later have to incarnate in another human body; or else it can leave the system altogether and attain perpetual liberation from rebirth. Both believe, moreover, in the eventual liberation of all souls. The Pythagoreans, who were a sect of Orpheus' school, held that at the end of a Great Year all were restored to their primal purity in a Golden Age, as the whole of Creation rejoins its source. The final destiny of all humanity – indeed of all creatures – is therefore the realization of Divinity. The Mystery initiate differs from the others simply in moving consciously towards that goal.

xvi *The Realm of Dionysus.* Wall-painting in the Villa of the Mysteries, Pompeii, late first century BC.

I *The Roman Gods*

The established religion of Rome was rather like the traditional Church of England: a solemn but unmystical affair, respectable yet undemanding of personal enthusiasm or spiritual effort. It supported the institutions of the family and the State by stressing rectitude in the performance of sacred and secular duties alike. Every paterfamilias was the Pontifex Maximus of his household, and every daughter a Vestal Virgin at her own hearth. Piety towards the gods was reflected in filial piety, the microcosm of the family corresponding to the macrocosm of Rome and the megacosm of a rather small universe. Such a religion considers the gods unphilosophically, intimately, as beings slightly larger than life who respond to human appeals. It seeks its rewards in this life on earth, considering death to be the end, to all intents and purposes, of the individual's existence. For after death comes Dis, a gloomy underworld in which the shades hover around, neither happy nor particularly sad, the semi-conscious husks of worn-out lives. No need, then, to enshrine the dead after the Egyptian or Etruscan fashion in cheerfully furnished and frescoed tomb-houses: for shades cannot appreciate such things.

A cold and prosaic affair was the old Roman faith, established at the behest of Jupiter himself by the legendary King Numa, for the preservation of the status quo among men and gods. Jupiter, Mars, Janus, Quirinus and Vesta formed the original pantheon, the Dii Indigetes, and a separate cult honoured the sun, Sol Indiges, as another of Rome's protectors. Together they ruled the obvious affairs of everyday life, such as war, weather and the home. For some people, then as now, such a religion – or none – sufficed. But it lacked any conception of the Absolute, had no real Mother Goddess, and held out no hopes for an after-life. In the following chapters we will consider some of the alternative and supplementary religions that sprang up in response to the spiritual needs which this quotidian faith could not satisfy.

Foreign goddesses were the first to arrive: Astarte-Atargatis from Phoenicia during the First Punic War (264–241 BC), Cybele in 204 BC, Isis by the first century BC. The Phoenician and East

Mediterranean religions had a strong irrational element, while the Egyptian ones appealed to intellectuals and aesthetes (Alexandria being the cynosure of both), and especially to middle-class women of the sort who nowadays practise yoga – another exotic cult. As devotion to these goddesses flourished, the establishment made efforts to Romanize their worship, purging it of excessively foreign elements (like yoga adapted for church-goers). Periodically these cults were altogether suppressed – Isis' five times at least between 59 and 48 BC. Yet Virgil, writing his political epic the *Aeneid*, could put Cybele's image on his hero's shield, so far was she accepted as the Great Mother of the Trojans and hence of Rome; and the bluff and soldierly Vespasian could sleep with his son Titus in the Roman Iseum. (One reads such things blandly in histories without always realizing that they would be comparable, say, to General Eisenhower making a retreat with the devotees of Krishna.)

Perhaps because their native religion was so uninspiring, the Romans were unusually tolerant of other men's faiths. Governments followed religious developments rather than instigating or hindering them, and suppressions and persecutions, when they occurred, were seldom unprovoked. The most severe assault on the Isiacs, for example, was prompted by the scandalous seduction of a respectable woman by a priest in the Roman Iseum. The persecutions of Christians and Jews generally followed their refusal to acknowledge the gods of Rome – a scruple that struck pagans as sheer obstinacy and, worse, a threat to the political cohesion of the Empire. If Alexander Severus could revere in his private chapel the statues of Apollo, Christ, Orpheus, Alexander and Abraham, why could not his subjects (whom, incidentally, he did not coerce) be similarly broad-minded?

But behind the tolerance and the syncretism lay a more profound quest, the search for an Absolute which could subsume all regional and aesthetic differences. There cannot be a Many without a One. On an official level this search eventually led through the deification of the Emperor himself to a solar monotheism. In the late third century AD Aurelian revived the old cult of Sol Indiges as 'Deus Sol Invictus': a supreme god who also synthesized Helios, Apollo, Mithras and all the Syrian Baals. The old religion of Janus, Quirinus, etc., already much shaken by the success of the Oriental cults, never survived the promotion of Aurelian's solar hierophants above the traditional priests of Rome, and the last battle of the ancient faiths was fought not by Mars but by the hosts of the Unconquered Sun under Licinus, against the Church Militant under Constantine.

1 *The Fall of the Titans*
Sarcophagus, second century AD. Vatican
Museum.

Before the Olympian Gods were born, the
Titans reigned, first-born of Heaven and
Earth. Jupiter conquered them after they
had devoured his son Dionysus Zagreus,
and from their ashes he made mankind.
Since the Titans had consumed the flesh of
the God, mankind contained a divine spark
in his gross, titanic body, which could be
realized and released through the Mystery
initiations. Appropriately enough, then,
these hybrid beings decorate a tomb, their
upper parts noble even in defeat, their
lower, divided selves a squirming mass of
reptiles.

2 *Jupiter in the Zodiac*
Sculpture from the Villa Albani, second
century AD. Vatican Museum.

The Father of Heaven, head of the Roman
pantheon and ruler from Olympus of both
gods and men, is Jupiter Greatest and Best
(Jupiter Optimus Maximus). He is a deity
of, and above, the whole cosmos, which is
his creation: hence this image of him as a
'universal' god whose power is central to
the visible world – the world of the Zodiac
supported by Atlas, and of day and night
figured as the torchbearing Dioscuri beneath
his throne. The planet Jupiter is one of his
lower manifestations, while to limited,
empirical vision the All-Father manifests as
a sky god, ruling the weather and wielding
his thunderbolt.

The peoples of the East whose theology
depended from a single all-powerful being –
whether imagined as a sky god or as a
metaphysical principle – saw in Jupiter the
Roman equivalent of their Lord, whence his
many adaptations to other cults and
countries, as Jupiter Haded at Baalbek,
Jupiter Dolichenus in Commagene, Jupiter
Sabazius in Anatolia. Through this
syncretism he took on characteristics far
removed from those of the
anthropomorphic Zeus of Greek
mythology, becoming steadily closer to the
solemn and inscrutable Jewish or Christian
father god. The corresponding decline in his
intimacy with man was made good by the
mediation of various saviours who bridged
the gap between mankind and the Most
High, Jupiter Exsuperantissimus.

Although Jupiter had no Mysteries
dedicated to him, he is in a way the *raison
d'être* of all the Mysteries, and the Father, in
some sense, of most of their founders.

41

3 *Diana-Luna*

Mosaic from the Tepidarium of the Oceanus Baths, Sabratha, first century AD. Libya, Sabratha Museum.

'Queen and huntress, chaste and fair . . .' Ben Jonson thus epitomized the paradoxical nature of Luna: ruler over fertility, she is herself sterile: seductive in her beauty, she is nevertheless a killer, as Actaeon found when he came too close. Her waxing and waning alternately encourage growing things and blight them, as old farmers know. The Moon sphere is also the first stage of the journey to higher worlds: souls go there after leaving earth, and fall from thence into new earth-lives. This is another manifestation of Luna's dual nature, presiding over birth and death in the sublunary realm.

4 *Venus with Nymphs*

Relief from Coventina's Well, High Rochester, Northumberland, second or third century AD. Newcastle-on-Tyne, Museum of Antiquities.

When Venus travelled with the legions to the North of England, she found herself already worshipped there in a triple form as Brigit, an aspect of the Great Mother Goddess. Like Luna, she is the bringer of fertility to plants, beasts and men, and since without water there can be no corporeal life as we know it, she appropriately rises, like the vegetative principle itself, from the waves. Her attendants – or her other forms – bear basket and pitcher, symbols of plenty, and perhaps allude to Venus' appearance in the sky as both the Morning and the Evening Star.

5 *Aesculapius, Apollo and Centaur*
Wall-painting from the House of Adonis,
Pompeii, first century A D. Naples, National
Museum.

The Greek god of healing, Asklepios
(Latinized to Aesculapius), was a son or
avatar of Apollo who was raised and
educated by the wise centaur Chiron. If the
myth of the centaurs derives from the wild
Thessalian tribes, whose horsemanship made
them seem inseparable from their mounts,
then Asklepios may well have been an actual
'hero' who learnt his lore from some
shamanistic tribesman. But this is a
euhemeristic interpretation, and discounts
the reality, known by all true healers, of a
healing force of Nature which can be
invoked and channelled – the *vis medicatrix
Naturae*. Asklepios then represents the

Spirits of Healing who work constantly to
balance our sickly condition.

The principal sanctuary of Asklepios was
at Epidaurus, with important centres also at
Athens, Pergamum and Cos, at which both
physical and psychic healing took, and still
takes place. One of the favoured cures was
incubation: sleeping overnight in the sacred
precinct, the sufferer benefited in sleep from
the healing forces, and was often rewarded
by a dream-message from the god. This
would be the equivalent of the 'big dreams'
that come to shamans, and also to modern
people, around which understanding and
future development crystallize. Aelius
Aristides, writing in the second century A D,
has left a full account of his own 'analysis'
through devotion to the Asklepios of
Pergamum.

43

6 *Aesculapius on Tiber Island*
Medal of Antoninus Pius, second century
AD. London, British Museum.

In 293 BC a pestilence attacked Rome.
Consultation of the Sibylline Books
brought the advice that Asklepios be
brought from Epidaurus. A brief embassy
was sent forthwith: it is not known what it
did, or brought back, but the plague seems
to have ceased. Two years later the Romans
fetched the god more formally, incarnated
in a serpent. On approaching Tiber Island,
the creature slipped from the ship and swam
to shore, and the Romans, always sensitive
to omens, built their Temple of Aesculapius
on that island. To this day there is a hospital
and a church there, dedicated to his
Christian reincarnation, St Bartholomew.

Under the influence of subsequent
spiritual currents in the Empire, Aesculapius
was regarded as a mediator of a more
general kind between man and a distant,
impersonal god, filling the role of a saviour
who heals not only sickness but the soul. He
appears on yet another level in the Hermetic
writings as one of the sons instructed by
Hermes. But whether as god, saviour or
disciple, he is a compassionate figure,
offering to his devotees the wisdom,
medical or occult, which removes the
obstacles to their progress. His attribute, the
serpent-entwined staff, correspondingly
symbolizes both the subtle currents of the
body and the spiral windings of the soul's
evolutionary path.

7 *Oceanus*
Mosaic from Hadrumentum, AD 150–200.
Tunisia, Sousse Museum.

A gigantic head, decked with seaweed and
crowned with crabs' pincers and corals,
arises dripping from the main. All around
are fish and crustaceans, showing the riches
of a realm which the Romanized Africans of
Susa could still, like Homer, call
'unharvested'. Oceanus is a member of the
primeval trinity, the son of Heaven
(Uranus) and Earth (Gaea). He stands for
the actual ocean with which ancient
geography encircled the earth, for the
magnetic field which some ancient Sages
knew to surround the earth, and for the
oceanic possibilities of a world yet
unformed and void, like the Waters of
Genesis. In man he arouses the feelings of
stupendous depth and breadth associated
with the open sea: an experience of
impersonal vastness so tangible as to be
frightening.

8   *Zodiac, Tellus, Seasons*
Mosaic from Sentinum, third century A D.
Munich, Glyptothek.

The late Hellenistic and Imperial periods
saw the rise to favour of several classes of
intermediate divinities: the Muses, Sirens,
Hours, Graces and Seasons. The latter,
stationed at the four corners of the earth and
of the year, impose a fixed scheme upon the
circular matrix of planetary revolution.
They symbolize the perfection of the
quaternity, as manifested in the cycles of
time (cf. the Hindus' four Yugas) and the
directions of space.

Tellus (Earth) surrounded by the Seasons
was used in the early Empire as an allegory
of the peace, plenty and harmonious order
that a *Pax Augusta* had brought to the
world. The male figure without attributes
may be Chronus (Time), turning the circle
of the Zodiac. But in the context – for this
mosaic comes from a Mithraic temple – he
may rather be the Sun, husband of the
Earth, whose fertilizing power as he
journeys through the Zodiac and the
Seasons, makes her fruitful. The feeling is
one of Earth and Heaven forming a single
happy family.

9　*The Seasons*
Sarcophagus, *c.* AD 300–20. Washington, D.C., Dumbarton Oaks Collection.

The Mystery religions recognized that a better fate awaits the dead than an eternity of zombie-like wandering in Dis. The journey through the spheres to a world metaphorically situated above the fixed stars was the goal of human life (see Introduction), and this is the hope expressed by the imagery on many sarcophagi of the later Empire. Like the Jupiter of Pl. 2 and many other figures (Pls 8, 50, 63, 75, 139, 142) the portraits of the deceased, man and wife, are framed by a Zodiac, meaning that they are elevated after death to a cosmic status. Very likely they were devotees of Dionysus, for the vintage scene beneath them shows frolicking putti pressing the intoxicating 'spirits' from the body of the grape: a clear symbol of the extraction of the soul from the body.

The Seasons who stand like heraldic supporters are reminders of the cosmic law and perfect harmony that reign in the beyond. Winged boys are also symbols of love, and death. Winter, dressed in Phrygian costume, is none other than Ganymede, the Phrygian shepherd-boy beloved and abducted by Zeus to become the wine-pourer of Olympus and the winter constellation of Aquarius. If the other Seasons had not lost their arms and attributes we might have been able to differentiate them, too. Both Hypnos and Eros were depicted as winged youths, summoners to the beyond whether through the sleep of death or the aspirations of the lover. Such figures are at the same time – most obviously in the case of Ganymede – symbols of the soul itself, imaged in the purity of youth, which is seized by the rapture of divine love, or flies heavenwards on its own wings.

10 *Pan and Hermaphrodite*
Wall-painting from Pompeii, first century A D. Naples, National Museum.

The horror of Pan on discovering that this beautiful woman is in fact a hermaphrodite is 'the rage of Caliban not seeing his own face in the mirror'. In Platonic terms, the pure, integrated oneness of the Soul is an apparition too fair for the bestial ego to behold. Both characters belong to the twilight world of satyrs, fauns, centaurs and sileni, who according to venerable tradition once thronged the globe, and whose descendants may still be glimpsed by the sensitive. These earlier stages of human evolution, the androgynous and semi-animal states, are recapitulated in the womb. So for an initiate of the Mysteries who had learnt of the true prehistory of mankind, this scurrilous scene would have held serious meanings.

11 *Deities of Delos*
The Corbridge Lanx, silver, fourth century A D. London, British Museum (on loan).

This family group includes the titaness Leto, her children Apollo and Artemis, and her sister Asteria who was transformed into the island of Ortygia, i.e. Delos, birthplace of the god and goddess. Athena joins them by virtue of the Athenians' long interest in the island. The motive for decorating this magnificent ritual tray with Delian divinities was probably the Emperor Julian's sacrifice to Apollo on the island in AD 363, before he left for his last campaign against the Persians. Its grandeur of conception and weakness of design seem to reflect the general loss of faith in the old gods, and Julian's almost desperate efforts to revive their former splendour. One remembers his visit to another temple of his favourite god, at Daphne near Antioch, where he hoped to witness spectacular public celebrations at the annual festival. He found instead a single priest, preparing to offer a sacrifice of one goose.

II *Mythology*

Most people today are persuaded that in the distant past infant mankind gradually differentiated themselves from their animal ancestors, growing step by step in understanding and intelligence until *homo* became *sapiens* and was able to take a rational view of the world around him. Things that were not at first understood, like the stars and the seasons, psychological events, birth and death, were expressed in personifications of great beauty and archetypal power. Myths are these explanatory tales told by primitive men when their world was still young, their minds as yet unburdened by logical necessity, their concepts unfocused by the separation of subject and object, mind and matter, reason and fantasy. Even now, the spell of myths holds sway over our atavistic imaginations: they inspire artists, fill our dreams, and even govern our behaviour – for we are not so very different from our forebears.

Another view holds that prehistoric men were not all primitive. Granted, they had perceptions and beliefs that run counter to our own, but if any be incorrect it is not theirs but ours, with our false distinctions and our absurd reliance on logic without feeling. They told in myths not what they fumblingly surmised, but what they knew. Sometimes their knowledge was such as to be inexpressible in our abstracted tongue, and then we must rely on artists, or on intuition, to recreate it for us. The characters in the myths, moreover, are not mere personifications: many of them were real people, others daemons or gods who, in some instances, are still with us. But such is the law of correspondences, layer upon layer, in the universe, that what happens in the realm of the gods is reflected in the life of man and throughout nature. So the same drama is played out at every level, and the myth, wise beyond human telling, may be read as deeply or broadly as one cares to range.

Perhaps for that reason, the mythographers' purpose has been served best by those who have not interpreted the myths, but simply retold them, like most of the visual artists whose work is reproduced here. It is the storytellers who keep the myths alive, who teach them from generation to generation, so that they take root in the soul of

Everyman. People in traditional societies are all raised with mythological beliefs, and when these have not been tampered with they are the perfect structures for experience, revealing primordial truths to every epoch and race. They do their work beneath the surface of consciousness, instructing the soul on its origins, nature and destiny. Subtly they inform the mind, preparing it for the day when it no longer need be taught in parables.

The most important myths from the point of view of the Mystery religions are those that concern the descent and ascent of the soul itself. The inclination of the Neopythagoreans and Neoplatonists was to interpret most myths as such, in their fundamental meaning. Homer's *Odyssey*, for example, received such treatment from Porphyry, the whole tale being understood as the journey of a man's soul to its true home. Such an attempt to adapt mythology to the purposes of spiritual philosophy is looked down upon by modern philosophers and dismissed as a Neoplatonic 'phase', just as the philosophy of Plotinus and Proclus is regarded as a passing episode in man's search for truth. But here we come to the crux of the two attitudes to ancient history mentioned above: the view one holds of mythology will depend on one's estimation of the Sages of the past and of the primeval ancestors who composed the myths in the dawn of history. Are we wiser than them, or were they wiser than us? Are the myths the end-point of their understanding, or a legacy from which to begin our own?

12   *Io received by Isis at Canopus*
Wall-painting from the House of the Duke
of Aumale, Pompeii, first century AD.
Naples, National Museum.

A Greek legend, illustrated by a Roman
artist with Egyptian motifs: here the three
streams of ancient mythology meet. Io, a
priestess of Argive Hera, was beloved by
Zeus. The jealous Hera turned her into a
heifer, and placed her under the vigilance of
the hundred-eyed herdsman Argos. Hermes
was sent by Zeus to slay her gaoler, and Io
wandered far and wide until in Egypt she
was restored by her lover to human form.

As a cow-shaped figure from Egypt, she
was naturally identified with Hathor, the
cow aspect of Isis. Here she wears vestigial
horns as she is carried by the god of the Nile
into the presence of Isis and Harpocrates,
attended by hierophants. The story may
have inspired Apuleius' *Metamorphoses* (or
The Golden Ass), at the end of which the
hero's devotion to Isis rescues him from his
donkey form. In both tales the inner
meaning is the same: the normal human
condition is thought of as 'bestial' in
comparison to the state from which we
come, and to which we hope to return.

13 *Persephone carried off by Pluto*
Wall-painting from the Tomb of the
Nasonii, Via Flaminia, later third century
AD. London, British Museum.

Sir James Frazer rightly saw in the central
myth of the Eleusinian Mysteries an
allegory of the vegetation cycle, in which
Persephone is the power of fertility which
disappears underground in winter and
returns with the spring; but like all exoteric
commentators he was blind to the other
meanings, without which the ancients
would scarcely have taken the Mysteries as
seriously as they indubitably did. The stolen
goddess represents the soul, alternately
descending at birth for 'half a year' in the
'underworld' of bodily existence, and
returning at death to the familiar and
fruitful fields of her true home.

14 *Adonis*
Wall-painting in the House of Adonis,
Pompeii, *c.* first century AD.

As the local god of Byblos, Adonis was the
son-lover of the Great Goddess Astarte. His
death came from a wound inflicted by a
boar (the animal of winter), but like
Persephone he was permitted to return to
earth for half of each year, to be with his
beloved. Thus Adonis is a male vegetation
principle, while Persephone is a female one.
One's choice would depend on whether one
considered as primary the reproductive
powers of Nature, who reawakens every
spring, or the fecundating powers of the
Sun, who spends most of each winter day
visiting the Antipodes. Adonis' cult spread
from the Lebanon to Alexandria, Athens
and Rome, and was particularly popular
among women who, identifying with the
Goddess, would annually 'weep for Adonis',
then joyfully celebrate his resurrection.

< 15 *Narcissus*
Cast of a lost well-head from Ostia.
Copenhagen, Thorvaldsens Museum.

The metamorphosis of Narcissus at the pool
is another myth of the descent of the soul,
in which he is envisaged as falling right
down to the vegetative level, becoming a
flower. The soul looks down from heaven
and sees its own image mirrored in the
deceptive surface of matter. Entranced by
the sight, it rushes to embrace the image and
finds itself tumbling headlong into a watery
grave. When it comes to, it is rooted in the
cold earth, beautiful but unconscious.

53

16 *Cupid and Psyche*
Relief from the Capua Mithraeum, third
century A D.

Psyche (Soul) was a maiden so beautiful that
mortals began to worship her instead of
Venus. The jealous goddess sent her son
Cupid to inflame Psyche with love for some
lowly object: instead, he fell in love with
her himself, visiting her *incognito* by night
but forbidding her to behold his true shape.
Psyche's jealous sisters persuaded her that
her secret lover was a monster, so that she
disobeyed his command and, lighting a
lamp, looked on him sleeping. A drop of
hot wax fell on him: he woke and fled from
Psyche, abandoning her to his mother's
wrath. For an age she wandered bereft,
performing tasks and undergoing torments
by Venus, until at last Cupid returned to
save her and, in the end, to make her his
wife. The tale as told by Apuleius is one of
the most beautiful allegories of the descent
of the Soul and her redemption by the
Divine Lover. The devotee who offered this
votive statue must have known the meaning
of the myth, and probably identified Cupid
with Mithras. Psyche wears butterfly wings,
for she has emerged from the chrysalis of
her earthly existence to be led by Cupid, the
Psychopompos, to the alchemical marriage
of Soul with Spirit.

17　*Endymion and Selene*
Wall-painting from Herculaneum, *c.* first century A D. Naples, National Museum.

The love of gods and goddesses for mortals has a highly spiritual connotation, as in St John the Divine's description of himself as 'the Disciple whom Jesus loved'. The classical freedom from embarrassment enabled such relationships to be described in antiquity through the apt metaphor of sexual passion. So Venus loved Adonis, Zeus loved a long series of fortunate women, and Selene loved Endymion, to whom Zeus granted unfading beauty – and perpetual sleep. The Moon Goddess is a dangerous lover, for she can entrap one and prevent the development of consciousness – whether one regards this in the psychological context of a 'devouring mother' complex, or in the occult tradition of the Moon sphere as the first stage of cosmic ascent: a boundary that certain souls cannot easily breach, hence remaining stuck in the relative unconsciousness of the Earth sphere.

18　*Ulysses and the Sirens*
Mosaic from the House of Dionysus, Dugga, third century A D. Tunis, Bardo National Museum.

Homer's *Odyssey*, like the book of Genesis, has more meanings than appear on the surface. The tale of Ulysses' wanderings is an allegory of the progress of the soul through earthly life, passing through many hazards, lessons and temptations until at the end it rejoins its faithful spouse in the haven of Ithaca, a city symbolic of the soul's true home. The Sirens' song, according to Thomas Taylor, 'signifies alluring and fraudulent pleasures which charm the soul' (note on Porphyry, *De Antro Nympharum*). The sailors correspond to those who must simply block their ears with wax, i.e. avoid such temptations altogether. It is for them that moral commandments and prohibitions are made. Ulysses, as a stronger character, takes the risk of seduction but is 'restrained by the bands of philosophy', so that he can 'experience delight without resigning the empire of reason to its fascinating control'.

III *The Imperial Cult*

Rulers have always been considered closer to the immortals than ordinary men. They have special relationships with the gods, and themselves aspire to the ranks of demigods and heroes. Alexander the Great declared himself the son of Zeus–Ammon after his encounter with the god in the Syrian desert. Scipio Africanus felt himself directly inspired by Jupiter after visiting his temple on the Capitoline Hill. Perhaps in emulation of these great leaders, perhaps also because of the tide of the times, the Roman emperors tended periodically to accept, or to claim, divine honours. This meant that they had temples, sacrifices and prayers dedicated to them; and it meant, presumably, that worship of them when alive or dead would procure the same objects as worship of any of the immortals.

In part this was a return to the idea of the Sacred Kings who ruled in the ancient days of Rome, though after the Republic no one dared to use the hated title of *Rex*. The old belief that the health of a nation is tied to that of its king led in primitive cultures to the periodic replacement of the old king by a younger and more virile challenger. But the attitude from Alexander onwards is more metaphysical, for both he and the Romans were influenced by the Oriental concept of the sovereign as avatar. According to this, the king has a 'genius' or presiding spirit, as every man does – perhaps it corresponds most closely to what some call the guardian angel – but the king's genius is of a higher order, belonging not to the humble ranks of daemons and sprites but to the company of the gods themselves. 'To those from whom much is expected, much is given.' The same was claimed for the philosophers Socrates and Plotinus. The king may even be a god himself, descended to earth in a temporary physical body for the benefit of mortals. As much is claimed for Jesus. It is therefore not the emperor as man, nor his personality or ego, which is worshipped, but his guiding spirit.

The situation is closely paralleled in Tibet, whose Dalai Lamas are regarded as *tulkus* (incarnations) of Avalokiteshvara, Bodhisattva of Compassion. The Dalai Lama, besides being the spiritual head of the largest Gelupka sect, was until recently also the temporal ruler of the nation. Just so, the Roman emperor from Julius Caesar onwards was also Pontifex Maximus of the State religion, high priest or 'bridge-builder' between men and gods.

If an emperor, or anyone else, is thought of as having incarnated something divine, then it follows that after his death that divine influence lives on and continues to deserve reverence. The deification of emperors after their death is quite similar in this regard to the Roman Catholic procedure of canonization; only the word 'god' sticks in the throats of monotheists. The simple Italians of the early centuries A D doubtless thought of the deified emperors as benign figures inhabiting the Empyrean, ready to listen to the requests of mortals if suitably prompted by sacrifice, just as their modern descendants imagine the saints in heaven who respond to candles, prayers and oblations.

The first emperor to be deified, two years after his death, was Julius Caesar (who did not himself believe in personal immortality). If he had been succeeded by Mark Antony, the divinization of the emperor would have continued there and then, for Antony had entered Ephesus as 'Dionysus' to be received by ecstatic maenads, and at his triumph in 34 B C had outraged Roman custom by offering his spoils not to Capitoline Jupiter but to Cleopatra clad as Isis, casting himself in the saviour role of Dionysus or Osiris. But this divine couple attained immortality only in literature, for the victor of Actium, Octavian (Pl. 19) had little feeling for foreign cults. He preferred Apollo, and encouraged the old Roman worship of Sol Indiges – as he encouraged everything old and Roman – by refounding the Secular Games in which the four-horse chariots raced like the Sun around the great obelisk of Seti I in the Circus Maximus.

After Augustus, most of the early emperors were led as much by public opinion as by their own tastes to support the Egyptian cults and accept a quasi-pharaonic role. Caligula of course revelled in the more bizarre aspects such as holy incest, dressing up statues, and ostentatious mourning. Claudius thought the cult of the Great Mother Cybele preferable to the Egyptian cults, but failed to make it the universal religion of the Empire. The solid Vespasian became a devotee of Serapis after a miraculous cure and vision in Alexandria. Domitian, after the priests of Isis had saved his life, built huge temples for the goddess, dressed as Osiris and adopted Egyptian dietary laws. It was he who first received the address of 'lord and god' (*dominus et deus*) while still alive. Trajan was too much of a soldier to have much interest in the rather theatrical rites of the Egyptian cults, but even he is shown on his triumphal arch sacrificing to Isis and Harpocrates. Such general acceptance of Egyptian ideas, together with the practice of posthumous deification, persisted through the reigns of the second-century 'good emperors' Hadrian (Pl. 22), Antoninus Pius (Pl. 23) and Marcus Aurelius (Pl. 41).

Marcus' stoic pessimism prevented him from indulging in such ideas himself, but it had little effect on his subjects as a whole. Commodus showed the lengths to which divine aspirations could push a man in his position. A religious dilettante, he observed Egyptian ceremonies, had a *taurobolium*, took part in the initiations of Mithras where he accidentally killed a man, and believed himself to be Hercules. He was murdered when on the point of demonstrating his herculean gifts by fighting in the Circus as a gladiator. After Septimius Severus (Pl. 24) and Caracalla (Pl. 25), the fourteen-year-old Syrian priest Elagabalus used the Imperium to push the cult of his own version of the Sun God at the expense of all others. His aspiration for one faith, one god, and one priest-king was a worthy one, but quite unworkable in practice, in the terrible third century, and dubious in theory so long as the priest-king was someone so unstable.

After fifty years of political turmoil Aurelian (Pl. 26) revived Elagabalus' solar monotheism as a means of unifying the Empire under himself as avatar of the Unconquered Sun God. Diocletian followed suit, an avatar this time of Jupiter, while his co-ruler Maximian was 'Hercules'. Constantine was another sun-emperor, who replaced the head of the colossal Helios in the Forum with his own, and flattered himself on his divine gift for searching the hearts of men. When after AD 323 it became politically expedient to enrol the Christians on his side, he had no trouble in changing his allegiance to the creator of the visible sun, nor in persuading the bishops to accept him as a chosen 'Man of God', the receiver of frequent personal visitations from above. Eusebius compared Constantine on his throne to God enthroned on the vault of heaven, and such similes persisted for centuries in the Eastern Empire, giving the theme to the entire Byzantine court ritual.

Constantine was the last of the god-emperors. Julian, who revived the solar worship for a brief Indian summer, was too Hellenic to take himself with the requisite seriousness, and after the Christianization of the Empire, both Eastern and Western rulers had to make at least a token obeisance to the new divinity of Christ. Examples from later history, however, show the same impulse working periodically in the inflated imaginations of rulers: the Emperor Maximilian planning to retire to the Papacy and die as a saint; Napoleon seizing the imperial crown from the Pope's hands and putting it on his own head; Hitler devising creeds and rituals for his master race.

19 *Octavian as Thoth-Hermes*
Stucco relief from the Farnesina, 30–25 BC.
Rome, National Museum.

Among the decorations of the Roman villa
excavated near the Farnesina is a group of
gods who include this portrait of Octavian,
later the Emperor Augustus, in the guise of
Thoth, Graeco-Egyptian god of wisdom.
Thoth, identified with the Greek Hermes
and Roman Mercury, was fabled to have
brought the Egyptians their letters, learning,
medicine, and all the accoutrements of
higher civilization. In the Augustan age it
seemed for a time that the Emperor was
restoring these gifts to a Rome wracked by
civil war.

Augustus himself was an initiate of the
Eleusinian Mysteries and a devotee of
Apollo, even regarded by some as an
incarnation of the Sun God. It was under his
rule that Apollo was first admitted within
the exclusive precinct of the Pomerium,
with a splendid temple built in 28 BC on the
Palatine Hill. At the same time Augustus
expelled from the inner city those Oriental
cults which had no traditional place in the
old Roman religion, believing that the new
Age of Gold for which his subjects yearned
could only be founded on the solid heritage
of the past.

20 An Early Emperor as Triptolemus
Silver patera from Aquileia, first century
AD. Vienna, Kunsthistorisches Museum.

Another emblem of the ruler as bringer of
gifts to his people is this identification of an
early emperor with Triptolemus, the mortal
to whom Demeter first revealed the secrets
of agriculture and fertility. Resembling in
design the Tazza Farnese (Pl. 95), this plaque
shows Jupiter in the sky watching the
Emperor sacrificing to the seated figure of
Demeter. Placed diagonally, the four
Seasons attend him; three children assist in
the sacrifice, and at the bottom Tellus and a
cow recline comfortably. As to the
identification of the emperor, Caligula,
Claudius and Nero have all been suggested.
Although none of them were initiated into
Demeter's Mysteries at Eleusis, the
graecophile Nero would have most
welcomed the identification with
Triptolemus.

21 Nero as High Priest of Apollo
Roman coin, c. AD 60. London, British
Museum.

Nero's love of art and Greek culture would
have made for a happier reign had he not
been encouraged by terrified sycophants
into excesses of egotism. His morally
unscrupulous and sentimental nature made
him unequal to the demands of the
Imperium. Yet, although the Persian
flatterer Tiridates addressed him as 'Mithra',
'Tyche', 'Moira', he never claimed to be a
god, only a universal genius. His cosmic
throne-room, which, if reports are true, had
a revolving ceiling that moved with the
heavens, was the centre of the Roman
universe; and if not a devotee of Apollo in
the religious sense, Nero's natural deity was
the leader of the Muses, patron of the arts,
and director of the cosmic dance.

22 Hadrian and Serapis
Roman coin, c. AD 120–30. London, British
Museum.

Everything Egyptian appealed to Hadrian,
most romantic of the emperors. He loved
the mysterious side of the Egyptian religion,
the temples and gardens, the gods and the
deified pharaohs. The god Serapis, lord of
Alexandria, stood for that blend of Greek
and Egyptian culture which Hadrian
admired, and on this coin he concurs with
the Emperor in dedicating an altar to the
Imperial cult. It was a time when peace
reigned, and even the Christian Patriarch
would worship Serapis as well as Christ
when he visited Alexandria. Hadrian had an
Egyptian water-garden and Serapeum built
at Tivoli, and statues of Isis in Hellenized
style decorated his new villa there. After his
lover Antinous was drowned in the Nile,
the beloved's body was celebrated in
numerous sculptures and his soul elevated to
godhead by Imperial decree: an honour
bestowed upon Hadrian himself after his
death.

23 *Apotheosis of Antoninus Pius and Faustina*
From Antoninus Pius' column, AD 160–1.
Vatican, Cortile della Pigna.

Antoninus earned his surname by his piety
in deifying his adopted father Hadrian, and
fully deserved it for the twenty-three years
of peace he brought to Rome. Upon his
death he was immediately deified, and this
column erected. The magnificent winged
figure combines the attributes of Aion
(Eternal Time) with those of the beautiful
Eros-Hypnos-Thanatos, the winged boy
who leads souls to the 'beyond', in any
sense. Eagles hover as attendant spirits,
indicating that the family of gods to which
the Emperor now belongs is that of Jupiter.
Rome and Egypt bid farewell.

24 Septimius Severus and Julia Domna sacrificing
Rome, Arch of the Argentarii, AD 203–4.

Septimius Severus was born in Libya, married a Syrian priestess, visited Egypt and died in York. His inner world seems to have been as vivid as his outer. He understood astrology and had his own horoscope painted on the ceiling of his courtroom (compare Nero's revolving dome). Once he dreamed that four eagles were bearing him heavenwards, and even in his lifetime he accepted assimilation to Serapis, returning from Egypt with his hair trained in Serapean forelocks. His empress Julia Domna came from the family of the high priest of Elagabal in Emesa, and accompanies him here with a gesture of prayer as he officiates as Pontifex Maximus. The Emperor and Empress have a triple function as rulers, hierophants and deities: in the latter function, they are Jupiter-Serapis and Juno Caelestis, descended to guide and enlighten their mortal subjects. Perhaps a figure of Hermes was originally planned to stand on the Empress's left, but only his caduceus carved. If so, he would have been an appropriate partner as the guide of souls and the bringer of good fortune, the twin objects of religious ritual.

25 Caracalla as the Infant Hercules
Statue, *c*. AD 195. Rome, Capitoline Museum.

As the oldest son of Septimius Severus, Caracalla carried high hopes from his birth. Here he is shown as the infant hero who strangled in his cradle the two serpents sent to kill him by Hera: perhaps an apotropaic gesture against the fates that sometimes befall young heirs. On his accession, Caracalla followed his father in devotion to Serapis, appearing on his coins as 'Serapis Cosmocrator', calling himself 'Philosarapis' and leading the Egyptian cults to their zenith.

26 Aurelian with Solar Crown
Roman coin, AD 270–5. London, British Museum.

Aurelian was the ultimate Sun King, combining the avataric function of Akhnaton with the pride of Louis Quatorze. He was the first emperor officially to be called 'Deus' while still alive, and his god was the Unconquered Sun. His mother had been a priestess of the Sun God in Pannonia, and when Aurelian came to fight the troops of Zenobia in the Syrian desert the god gave him victory. He never faltered from then on in his devotion, but unlike other monotheists was wise enough to accept all other gods as aspects of the Supreme. He built for the Sun splendid temples, instituted games, established a college of priests parallel to that of the old Roman gods (heading both colleges as Pontifex Maximus), and unified the Empire both politically and religiously.

IV *Magical and Folk Beliefs*

The exoticism of the Oriental religions and the snob-appeal of the Imperial cult held little attraction for the conservative Italian peasantry. They lived, nevertheless, in a universe thronged with immaterial beings whose anger or favour must be considered at every turn. Superstition is the philosophy of the peasant, and magic his Mystery religion. Neither is to be despised, any more than his age-old wisdom of root and branch, wind and weather, seed-time and harvest. Folk beliefs and folk art often contain doctrines and symbols of an authentic kind, deriving from the primordial revelation to the race, and they often preserve ideas in all their purity long after 'fine' art has abandoned them to chase its own aesthetic chimeras. Fairy tales are one example of this (consider the tale of Sleeping Beauty, for instance, as a myth of the soul's descent and rebirth); geometrical art, with its spirals and swastikas, is another. Unfortunately for us, the materials of peasant art are usually organic and ephemeral (wood, cloth), in contrast to the official media of bronze and stone, so comparatively little of it has lasted from antiquity.

These plates show mainly middle-class artefacts, but ones which are informed by beliefs common to the folk as a whole: beliefs in witches, fairies and hobgoblins, in gnomes of the garden and ghosts of the dead. The strains of black and white magic intertwine, shading off into a kind of grey magic which, while not usually vicious in intent, still serves only the earthly interests of the operator. Some would see evidence here of what they call the Old Religion, of the god of the witches with whom we associate phallicism, sympathetic magic, spells and charms. Others would identify these Lares and Lemures with the Spirits of Place, with subterranean currents, dragon lines and the like. Both are right in their own way, for the folk have always known something of both realms: the sublunary spirits and the energies beneath the earth. The co-operation of both is necessary before the humblest weed can sprout, and without them both peasants and patricians would have long ceased to eat.

27 *Offering to Priapus*
Altar from Aquileia, first century A D.
Aquileia, Museo Nazionale.

Priapus is a god of fertility, and his
attributes are fruits and his phallus. He is a
simple deity, and loved by simple people
whose life and livelihood depends on the
fertility of plant and beast. To him it is
appropriate to offer one's first fruits, in
expectation of obtaining an abundance in
return. The old devotee here seems to be
receiving the sacrificial fire from the source
of life itself.

28 *Priapus*
Terracotta lamp from Pompeii, *c.* first
century A D. Naples, National Museum.

Priapus' excessive virility has another,
aggressive side to it, which in our unmagical
times surfaces only in slang expressions. This
homunculus is designed to be hung up in a
doorway, his phallus aflame, telling evil
spirits and other undesirables in no uncertain
terms to 'f—— off'!

29 *Ivy-wreathed Herm*
Bronze herm, allegedly from Konya, first
century A D. University of Pennsylvania
Museum.

The herm or terminal god originated as a
mere pillar, marking boundaries and other
important spots. With the tendency of such
stones to become personified, it was natural
for the head to be added, and the phallus
completes the anatomy with the idea of
drawing cosmic forces creatively into the
earth – another function of sacred stones.
Garlanding and wreathing the stones with
evergreens encourages their double guardian
and fecundating function. So all the features
are reproduced in miniature on this bronze,
doubtless designed for some house shrine.

30 *Lar*
Bronze statuette from Herculaneum, *c.* first
century A D. Naples, National Museum.

This Lar carries a sheaf of wheat and a wine
bucket, symbols of the two basic foodstuffs
for bodily and mental well-being. He looks
like a young slave, perhaps incorporating
the idea of the beneficent elf or friendly
gnome common in fairy tales who helps in
the household and secretly aids the heroine.

31 *Altar of the Lares*
Wall-painting from Pompeii, first century
AD. Naples, National Museum.

Pious Romans must have lived in a universe
populated by unseen divinities of house and
hearth, some friendly in aspect like these
two Lares, others awe-inspiring like the
gigantic serpents in the lower register. The
sacrifice of a pig is about to take place, to
the raw sound of double pipe (aulos) and
foot-clapper. The Lares dispense their life-
giving liquor with more panache than good
aim, and the chthonian spirits, kept in their
place underground, approach to feast on the
victim's life force, symbolized by the
testicles.

32 *Sacrificial Ram on Altar*
Statue of unknown provenance. London, British Museum.

The careful carving of a dead ram shows the respect in which the practice of sacrifice was held in antiquity. Apart from the symbolic offering of the animal's life force on behalf of the sacrificer, the ritual slaying afforded an opportunity for divination. Haruspicy (divination from examining the entrails of the victim) was a valued source of revelation: from the condition of the entrails could be judged the success or otherwise of whatever venture had prompted the sacrifice. Roman history is full of events predicted in this way, some of them no doubt self-fulfilled prophecies, but others genuine instances of magical precognition.

33 *Charm of Solomon*
Bronze medal, fifth century AD or later. University of Michigan.

'Whosoever dwelleth under the defence of the Most High, shall abide under the shadow of the Almighty' (Psalm 91). 'To God be victory over evil.' 'Holy, holy, holy Lord of Sabaoth.' 'The seal of the Living God is mixed with this amulet to protect against all evil.'

With such quotations, we clearly have an object designed to ward off supernatural influences, personified in the lion-woman whom 'Solomon' (as he is styled in similar designs) is spearing. On the obverse is Christ in Majesty between the four beasts, a lion and a crab, and symbols which resemble closely the sigils of the planets in later grimoires. The whole is a synthesis of Christian, Jewish and astrological magic, and the design anticipates the later iconography of St George and the Dragon, and Perseus and Andromeda.

34 *Triple Hecate*
Stele from Constantinople, second–third
century AD. London, British Museum.

Hecate is the Great Goddess in her darker
and more sinister aspects: the goddess of
graveyards, crossroads and nocturnal
conjurations. According to Plutarch, the
Moon is the domain of both a chthonic and
a uranian Hecate, meaning that the
particular power which she represents exists
in earth, moon and sky, the domains of the
three Fates. Alternatively she can be seen as
a goddess of the Moon alone, in the three
phases originally ascribed to her: waxing,
full and waning. In either case she reigns
over maleficent forces, and it is as well to be
on good terms with her.

35 *The Sacred Betyl entering Rome*
Gold aureus of Elagabalus, *c.* AD 225.
London, British Museum.

The power of many of the East
Mediterranean gods was incarnated in
sacred stones: sometimes meteorites,
sometimes hewn or unhewn rocks. The
archaic obelisks of Byblos still stand as
monuments to the spirits of that place,
captured like Ariel in Prospero's cloven
pine. But the meteoric stone or 'betyl' of
Emesa was a movable home for what its
high priest, Elagabalus, considered the
Supreme Deity; so when he became
emperor he had it moved to Rome. It
entered the city mounted like all triumphant
gods on a four-horse chariot (see also Pls 50,
83, 103, 121, 139), and no one could deny
that it brought the most extraordinary
influences with it, leading Rome to anarchy
and chaos. Alexander Severus, who
succeeded Elagabalus' short and disastrous
rule, probably did wisely to send back the
betyl to Emesa and rid the city of its sinister
power.

V *Philosophers*

The culture of the classical age of Greece owed its peculiar quality and greatness to the precarious, knife-edge balance which its artists and thinkers were able to maintain between the material and spiritual worlds, each informing the other, neither side avoided or overemphasized. When the Hellenic epoch drew to a close in the first century B C, the equilibrium was broken, and even the best efforts to revive it were thereafter no more than artificial respiration. The philhellenic emperors Hadrian and Julian only succeeded, like the Gothic Revivalists, in an earnest but lifeless pastiche of the original. The lightness and life had gone from the Greek forms, because the spirit had departed, leaving aspiration without insight, technique without *sprezzatura*.

In philosophy the reaction was for the two sides of the balance to part company. On the one hand there flourished superstition, an unintelligent star-lore and a simplistic magic; on the other, a rank scepticism. The lower manifestations of the Mystery religions abetted this imbalance, repelling the philosophical as they attracted the sensation-seekers. The consensus of belief was shattered, and nowhere so strikingly as in the variety of opinions which were now held, not just by contentious philosophers but by ordinary people, on the subject of the Soul.

Stoics and Epicureans had a neat and easy way of disposing of this problematic entity. They restricted their idea of a soul to the etheric body, the carrier of vital energy which man shares with the animal and even the vegetable kingdom. They held that this does not long survive bodily death, but decomposes along with the physical body and returns to its own 'dust', the ether, without rising above the sphere of the Moon. The Stoics accepted the existence of higher elements in man, such as the Fire of Reason, but believed that this also dissolves back into its universal source, leaving no individuality to experience any posthumous state. Stoic immortality – if one can call it that – occurs only as the eternal, cyclic return of all events in the Universe: some day, aeons hence, one will come again and lead the same life on the same earth. Stoicism is thus rather like a Buddhism without a Nirvana. Epicurean immortality is simpler still, lasting only so long as one is remembered upon earth. Epicurus himself rather pathetically enjoined his disciples to celebrate his monthly birthday after he was gone.

Aristotle also denied any happiness to the dead, allowing the Rational Soul (the highest element in man) an impersonal existence only. Yet even this was denied by some Peripatetics of the third and second centuries B C, such as the Aristotelian commentator Alexander of Aphrodisias, who 'proved' that both the rational and the animal soul die with the body; and if indeed death is the dissolution of personality, then this is certainly a logical conclusion. Given these dismal prospects, the best life one could be encouraged to live was a harmless one, avoiding what suffering and pursuing what pleasure one could.

When we turn to the Mystery religions and to the philosophers who provided their intellectual underpinning, things are very different. For all of them, on the exoteric level, the hope and expectation was that after death the Soul would be reunited with God and live for ever with him or her in boundless felicity. None would deny that the subtle bodies dissolve like corpses when they are vacated: but these are not confused with the Soul, or higher Self, which persists through death to live a new life. The famous tomb inscription, 'I was not – I became – I am no more – I do not care', probably refers to this doctrine: 'I', the lower ego embodied awhile in matter of various densities, is of no lasting concern.

An important point still remains, however. Does this new life of the Soul mark the end of striving, the end of individual effort, or is there more to come? The simpler philosophy is to draw the line then and there and to think no more about it: to assume that if one follows a prescribed path in life, one will go happily to Heaven. More profound thinkers cannot avoid asking awkward questions: what exactly is Heaven? What is the exact nature of the Soul? How can soul be a separate entity if it is one with the god? What god is it one with? Why was it in a body in the first place? Where did it come from? These are the questions asked, and answered, by the philosophers of the Pythagorean–Platonic tradition. They learned the answers not through reasoning alone but through initiation into the Mysteries. Without initiation or mystical intuition a philosopher is restricted to the narrow field of rational speculation in which he can only pace to and fro, like a caged lion, ignorant of what true freedom can be.

36 *Pythagoras* (*c.* 570–470 B C)
Bronze head from the Villa dei Pisoni,
Herculaneum. Naples, National Museum.

Born on the isle of Samos, Pythagoras
studied with the Greek philosophers
Pherekydes, Anaximander and Thales,
visited the Magi of Babylon and the
hierophants of Egypt, and returned to
found a school of spiritual science in
Crotona, south Italy. He is seldom credited
with his true rôle, which was to transplant
some of the esoteric wisdom of those
ancient and moribund civilizations into the
new soil of Greece, combining it with
elements of the Orphic tradition. His
philosophy sought above all to purify the
soul through revealed knowledge and
ascesis: thus his pupils had to undergo a
five-year period of unquestioning
instruction, and observe strict rules of
conduct.

37 *Socrates* (469–399 B C)
Antique copy of Lysippus' original
(*c.* 325 B C). Vatican Museum.

Socrates did not learn his philosophy
through the normal human channels, but
intuitively through intimacy with his
daemon or guardian spirit. In the portrait of
him which emerges from Plato's dialogues,
he shows all the qualities that one associates
with the Enlightened ones of Buddhism and
Hinduism: courage, compassion, humour
and inner peace. Socrates was the first
religious teacher in the West to encourage
doubt and the questioning of dogma,
trusting his pupils to reach their vision of
the truth and to conduct their lives on a
basis of their own inner convictions. In this
he contrasts strongly with the didactic
Pythagoras. Not a writer himself, he made
use of Plato's great literary powers to
immortalize his method of enquiry and his
ethical system.

38 *Plato* (*c.* 429–347 B C)
Antique copy of Silanion's original
(*c.* 370 B C). Holkham Hall, Norfolk.

Plato drew his wisdom from the twin
sources of Egypt and Socrates. Egyptian
science and mysticism he knew directly
through initiation there, and indirectly
through his friendship with Pythagoreans.
Through Socrates' influence, he was able to
present his incomparable system of
philosophy not as revelation but as a
reasoned argument. The dualities within
Plato's own work, such as those of spiritual
certainty versus logical enquiry, or
collective organization versus the
individual's quest, epitomize all the
problems and tasks of subsequent Western
civilization, from the political to the
mystical level.

40 *Arrival of a Soul in Elysium*
Stucco relief in the Porta Maggiore Basilica,
Rome, *c.* AD 50.

The heaven of the mystical philosophers
differed both from those of the Stoics,
Epicureans and Peripatetics (who had
none), and from the twilight existence
which was all that traditional Roman
religion offered the ordinary person after
death. Although there was not agreement as
to the exact part of the soul that survives
death, Pythagoreans, Platonists and every
Mystery cult concurred in envisaging death
not as an end but as a beginning to life on
another plane, perhaps more significant and
almost certainly more agreeable than our
present one. The reception of a soul in
'Elysium' is a solemn and joyous occasion,
at which the soul is personified as Ariadne
greeted by Bacchantes as she enters
Dionysus' own realm.

39 *Subterranean Basilica*
Beneath the Porta Maggiore, Rome.
c. AD 50.

This remarkable underground chapel was
discovered in 1917 beneath the railway line;
it seemed to have been abandoned almost as
soon as it was completed, with its
decorations of low stucco reliefs depicting
mythological scenes and characters. Its exact
purpose is unknown. Carcopino thought it
the actual 'church' of a Neopythagorean
congregation: Vermaseren interprets it as
most probably a funeral chapel or chantry.
In the place of honour on the apse is the
poetess Sappho, a favourite of the
Pythagoreans, who, driven to desperation
by her love for the ferryman Phaon, leapt
off the Leucadian rock into the sea (told in
Ovid, *Heroides* 15). In this context Sappho
represents the soul, living in 'poetic'
harmony, who in revulsion against excessive
attachment to the physical body takes the
leap into the sea of the unknown, either
though initiation or at actual death.

41 *The Stoic Emperor Marcus Aurelius*
(AD 121–80)
Bronze medallion, *c.* AD 170. London,
British Museum.

'Think on this doctrine: that reasoning beings are
created for one another's sake; that to be patient
is a branch of justice; and that men sin without
intending it.'
   'All that is harmony for thee, O Universe, is in
harmony with me as well. Nothing that comes at
the right time for thee is too early or too late for
me.'
   'You will find rest from vain fancies if you do
every act in life as if it were your last.'

from Marcus Aurelius' *Meditations*
(iv, 3, 23; ii, 5)

42   Epicurean Skeletons
Silver goblet from the Boscoreale Treasure,
first century B C. Paris, Louvre.

This shadow-play of corpses mocks those
who take seriously such doctrines as the
immortality of the soul, the existence of
heavens or hells, communication with the
gods. The disciple of Epicurus is urged to
do away with rites and superstition and to
'survey all things with a mind at peace'
(Lucretius, *De Rerum Natura* v, 1194 ff.).
'Suns may rise again, but ours is an eternal
sleep' (Catullus v, 4). One should be glad
that death will surely come: it is the greatest
boon, since there is no Hell to fear and no
consciousness beyond the grave. To his
disciples Epicurus was the equivalent of a
saviour god, having freed them from all fear
and given them rules for the conduct of a
good life – which are not, as it happens,
very different from those of the Stoics, since

they stress not gluttony and hedonism but
temperance and loyalty. True Epicureanism,
like Buddhism, teaches that the fewer
desires one has, the less one suffers the pain
of unsatisfied longing.

43   The Emperor Julian (A D 332–63)
Statue, A D 361–3. Paris, Louvre.

Julian 'the Apostate' forsook the semblance
of Christianity in which he had been
brought up, and when he unexpectedly
succeeded to the Imperium made it his life's
ambition to restore the worship of the
Gods. Unlike previous reforming emperors,
he was well versed in philosophy and
theology of the Neoplatonic school, and
himself (like all the Neoplatonists) an
initiate and a mystic. He encouraged the
revival of the lower forms of paganism,
such as sacrifice and theurgy (see
Introduction), only because he could
understand their metaphysical and
theological basis. For his own part, his
inclination was towards a solar monotheism
that recognized the visible Sun in the sky as
the lowest of a series of gods that reached
up, ultimately, to the Absolute One.
Unfortunately he died young in battle and
his reforms were almost immediately
dismantled.

44 *Apuleius of Madaura* (*c*. AD 123 – after AD 180)
Gold contorniate, second century AD. Paris, Bibliothèque Nationale.

Apuleius moved in fashionable circles as a poet, rhetorician and chief priest of the province of Carthage. He is one of the great worldly disciples of the initiatic tradition, who like Socrates and Julian could range from ribald humour to mystical ecstasy. The novel for which he is justly celebrated, entitled *Metamorphoses* or *The Golden Ass*, describes the fate of one Lucius who meddled with magic and was turned into a donkey. Lucius suffered and learned much in this form before he was restored to human shape through his devotion to Isis, receiving a theophany of the goddess and of Osiris that Apuleius recounts in one of the most persuasive descriptions of mystical experience to have survived from the ancient world.

45 *Philosophers and Muses*
Sarcophagus of Publius Peregrinus, *c*. AD 250. Rome, Museo Torlonia.

The philosopher is 'saved' not by a mediating divinity but by the elevation of his own soul through wisdom. In this sarcophagus Publius and his wife are assimilated to the Seven Sages and the Nine Muses: they themselves complete the traditional numbers. The Muses, guardians of wisdom, patronesses of the arts and sciences, are the teachers and inspirers of philosophers, and also, in late antiquity, the guides of the soul after death. There is some apt psychological symbolism in the attitudes of husband and wife: she personifies with her closed scroll Sophia, the innate possessor of all wisdom, while he exercises the masculine Logos as he reads from an open scroll. The feminine knows all things, yet looks to the masculine for rational understanding and verbal expression.

VI *Judaism*

The point at which canonical Judaism comes closest to the Mystery religions is in the Wisdom literature of the early centuries B C: *Koheleth* (Ecclesiastes), *Ben Sira* (Ecclesiasticus), *Chokmah* (Wisdom of Solomon), Proverbs, and the Book of Job. Here the Jewish perspective extends over the whole of humanity, dividing mankind not into Jews and Gentiles but rather into the Wise and the Foolish. The piety of the heart is stressed more than obedience to the Mosaic law, and Jehovah is seen as the Lord over the whole earth who has created and ordered all things visible and invisible.

This reformed Judaism developed primarily in Hellenistic Alexandria, where a large colony of Jews throve in easy commerce with people of other races. The Septuagint translation of the scriptures into Greek was made in the last centuries B C to serve those Jews whose first language was no longer Hebrew, and in the same climate of Hellenic and Egyptian influence some Jewish philosophers sought to reconcile their ancestral faith with the wisdom of other peoples. Some, following the rational principles of Aristotle and Euhemerus, questioned the fundamentalist attitude to the Pentateuch (the first five books of the Bible) and began to interpret them allegorically. When such allegorizing was applied, for example, to the Mosaic dietary laws, it threatened the whole structure of social customs which differentiate Jews from Gentiles. But despite such rapprochements with the world of the Diaspora, the one thing which the Jews would never abandon was their monotheism: 'Thou shalt have no other gods but me.' For those of the Palestinian revival under the Maccabees, 'me' signified the Jehovah who had given them the victory over their oppressor Antiochus Epiphanes, enabled them to expel from Jerusalem the hated cults of Olympian Zeus and Dionysus, and pressed them on to expand their territories. For the Alexandrian mystical philosopher Philo, 'me' was Ain Soph, the Absolute, devoid, like Plato's One or the Hindu Brahma, of all qualities whatsoever. This monotheism had always inclined the Jews to hold in contempt the gods which their neighbours worshipped, and such an attitude led in AD 38 to serious violence against them by the Greek citizens of Alexandria. Philo, no longer a young man, was chosen by his community as an emissary to Rome, like St Paul twenty years later, to petition the Emperor Gaius for exemption from observance of the Imperial cult.

It would be interesting to know how great a part has been played by language in the history of the monotheistic religions, because both Muslims and Christians have always been willing to accept as 'saints' and 'angels' those powers to which pagans give the names of 'heroes' and 'gods'; and the heaven of Philo's theology is full of angels, who like the Platonic Ideas or the Neoplatonic gods are contained in the mind of the Supreme One. The highest of these, subsuming all the others, Philo calls the Logos: the principle of reason and order through which God makes the universe. The Wisdom literature had already separated this concept as Chokmah, the Divine Wisdom; the Gnostics knew it in Philo's day as Sophia; St John the Evangelist was to identify it with the Christ. And at the same time the Kabbalists were analysing the levels of being in their own way, making Chokmah the second of the ten divine emanations whose scheme they set out as the Tree of the Sephiroth. When Kabbalists analyse the Pentateuch, breaking down the actual words into their numerical equivalents, they find metaphysical and cosmological doctrines concealed in the very letter of the Law. This suggests that whoever wrote those earliest Hebrew scriptures was already adept at understanding, and concealing, the most profound knowledge. 'Moses' – whether he was a single man, a succession of masters, or an esoteric school – learnt his lore from the sages of Egypt, and recast it in this form.

So beneath the surface of Judaism there has always been a strong Mystery content. Philo forbade his people to take part in pagan initiations, suggesting that there were Mysteries in their own faith to which they might aspire. Certainly the road is hard, and reserved for the few who have shown sufficient zeal in studying the Torah, the body of the Mosaic Law, and its formidable commentaries. As a result, most Jews remain to this day ignorant of their esoteric heritage, regarding it as a strange pursuit of the exceedingly Orthodox, unless they have been led by a more general interest in religion to learn what they can of it through books. Yet it cannot be denied that the Kabbalistic schools are the sole representatives of the Mystery religions that have continued uninterruptedly from the day of their foundation until the present.

46 *Menorah with the Seasons*
Fragment of sarcophagus from the Vigna
Rondanini catacomb, Rome, *c.* A D 300.
Rome, National Museum.

The Mosaic commandment against graven
images was not strictly observed in later
Judaism, as illustrated by this Hellenized
Jewish sarcophagus which with its
Dionysian vintage-scene and naked Winter
borrows from such pagan iconography as
that of Pls 9 and 100. The Seven-branched
Candlestick is a symbol of the Sun
surrounded by the six planets, and hence of
the journey the soul makes after death in all
the Mystery religions. Esoterically, the
Menorah also conceals the Kabbalistic Tree
of the ten Sephiroth, the system of divine
emanations that is the highest philosophical
achievement of Judaism.

 The enclosure of a god's image in the
circle of the Zodiac, found very frequently
in late antiquity (e.g. Pls 2, 8, 75), finds here
its Jewish equivalent in the circle held by
two Victories, on which is the impersonal
image of the Menorah.

47 *Anointing of King David*
Wall-painting (copy) from the Synagogue,
Dura Europos, *c.* A D 240. Original in the
National Museum, Damascus.

The anointing of a king from a horn of oil
is a magical act, bestowing on him the
'Divine Right of Kings' – which even David
later abused. As soon as Samuel anointed the
young David (I Samuel 16), the 'spirit of the
Lord' left Saul and descended upon him.
This is the Jewish way of describing what
the Romans would have called the
Emperor's 'genius', a psychic concomitant
of the power he wields in the material
world.

48   *Joseph and Solomon*
Silver reliquary, end of the fourth century
A D. Milan, San Nazaro Maggiore.

Both these Old Testament figures are
shown as judges, making the open-palmed
gesture of power. Joseph is pardoning his
brothers who sold him into Egyptian hands
(Genesis 45), and Solomon is calling the
bluff of the two women who both claim the
same infant (I Kings 3). In this probably
Christian reliquary they probably stand for
the twin function of Christ as Judge: on the
one hand Mercy, on the other Severity.
These names are given to the Sephiroth
Chesed and Geburah, and they represent the
workings of the Lord's will experienced
subjectively as rewards and punishments.

49   *Dish with Judaic Symbols*
Gilded glass from the Jewish catacombs,
Rome, fourth century A D. Jerusalem, Israel
Museum.

The main symbols are the open tabernacle
full of scrolls and the Menorah. Exoterically
these represent the revelation of Moses to
God's chosen people, and the lamp of faith
which Jews throughout the world keep
alight in their hearts. Esoterically they are
the Kabbalistic wisdom concealed, layer
beneath layer, in the first books of the Old
Testament; and the cosmic and
metaphysical order of the universe which
these books reveal to the learned Jew.

50 *Zodiac with Sun Chariot*
Mosaic from the Synagogue, Beth Alpha
(Israel), after A D 569.

Here is a Jewish adaptation of a favourite
pagan scheme: the twelve zodiacal signs
surrounding the Sun, with the four Seasons
or Winds forming a cross. The far-reaching
symbolism of the signs also lies behind the
twelve gems on the High Priest's breastplate
(Exodus 39) and the twelve gates of the
New Jerusalem (Revelation 21), while the
four Seasons are lower manifestations of the
four Apocalyptic Beasts (Revelation 4) or
Archangels who guard this earth.

VII *Gnosticism*

This most problematic of cults arose in Palestine in the first century BC – its exact origins are still disputed by scholars – and spread in the following century from a secondary centre in Alexandria. It was an extraordinary phenomenon: a religion of extremes, nurtured in the same atmosphere of apocalyptic syncretism into which Jesus came. In both Palestine and Egypt at the end of the Hellenistic age, unorthodox Jews mingled with Greek philosophers and Persian dualists; and somewhere in that confused but thrilling encounter Gnosticism was born, the religion of Gnosis – knowledge of the true nature of things. Of all the religions treated in this book, it is the most un-Roman: it needed the desert and the impetus of Oriental fanaticism. Decadent Alexandria was a more fertile soil for it than burgeoning Rome, but once it had taken root there, it put out adventitious sprouts of protean diversity all around the Mediterranean for four centuries and more.

The most radical tenet of Gnosticism is that the world is a stupendous mistake, created by a foolish or vicious creator-god. This creator or Demiurge is a god of a very low grade on the celestial hierarchy, himself the result of an error, who thinks that he is supreme. His pride and incompetence have resulted in the sorry state of the world as we know it, and in the blind and ignorant condition of most of mankind. The Gnostic, however, is not fooled. Although like every man he suffers under the tyranny of this monster, he knows that far above the Demiurge there is another God. He believes, moreover, that humanity is not totally without hope of reaching this true God whom the Demiurge does his best to hide, both from himself and from his subjects.

Given this fundamental attitude, Gnosticism is able to fasten like a parasite upon Platonism, Persian dualism or Christianity. The Platonists explain that from the higher gods emanate lower gods, in a vast hierarchy that stretches down from the One and the archetypal Ideas to the Demiurgic Jupiter, who made the planet we live on. The human soul, naturally a part of the higher planes, is sunk in matter and in ignorance, and its task is to journey laboriously upwards, leaving behind the world of substance to rejoin its native star, or even to be subsumed in the very Absolute itself. A Gnostic Platonist, such as Plotinus found cause to combat (*Enneads* 2, 9), would say that Jupiter was a tyrant and a usurper, and that all who challenged his powers (like the Titans, or Prometheus) deserved credit for looking above and beyond his miserable empire.

A Gnostic would also be sympathetic to the Persians, who saw the universe as the theatre for a perpetual battle between the powers of light and those of darkness. The Demiurge now becomes identified with Ahriman, the dark power, whose realm is matter; and Ahura Mazda, the God of Light, corresponds to the *Deus absconditus*, the hidden Supreme God. But the Gnostic by no means regards the two as equal: only on earth do the evil forces enjoy parity with, even superiority over, the good.

In respect to Judaism the Gnostics turn the whole Old Testament upside-down. Jehovah is the wicked Demiurge, and the whole testament is the story of his tyranny and egotism, as enforced on a people who were tricked into worshipping him as the Supreme God. An emissary of the true God appeared to Adam and Eve in the Garden of Eden as the Serpent, and taught them what wisdom they could learn before Jehovah expelled them into the utter darkness of 'ordinary life'. Thereafter, all the villains of Jewish history – Cain, Esau, the Sodomites, etc. – become heroes for resisting his persecution.

The advent of Christ was recognized by the later Gnostics as a cosmic event of the utmost magnitude. For at the Baptism, there entered into the body of Jesus of Nazareth the direct influence of the True God. Christ is *his* son, not Jehovah's, and a god in his own right from a level far above the Demiurge. He descended to teach men the only thing that will get them out of their appalling predicament: knowledge of the true state of affairs.

The utter contempt in which the Gnostics held the entire created world and its creator did not make for the encouragement of the arts. Very little of Gnostic literature or artefacts has come down to us, for these people simply did not see any point in creating fresh errors or in leaving memorials behind them. Nearly all that we know of their doctrines comes from what their opponents and detractors had to say about them. Perhaps the most straightforward is Marcion, born a bishop's son in AD 85 and called by St Jerome a 'veritable sage'. He worked to separate Christianity totally from its Jewish roots, regarding the Old Testament merely as a catalogue of the Demiurge's crimes against humanity. He has Jesus descend to Hell after the

Crucifixion to rescue the Old Testament 'villains' and all the Gentiles, leaving behind Abraham, Moses and all the other henchmen of Jehovah.

A similar *bouleversement* of accepted ideas is found also in the Gnostic ethical teachings, exemplified by Basilides' dictum: 'The perpetration of any voluptuous act whatever is a matter of indifference.' Basilides (early first century AD) and his successor Valentinus, the great masters of Alexandrian Gnosticism, favoured a strict amorality: the only rule was that there are no rules. If, as many initiates preferred, one's bent was ascetic, that was fine; if one was completely promiscuous, that was also fine: for the world is only an illusion in the brain of the non-God. Real life lies elsewhere, beyond human distinctions of good and evil. Some Gnostics, like Carpocrates, went further than Basilides' indifference and actually urged their followers to 'sin': to stoke the forbidden fires of desire so as to reduce them to ashes. They rejected private property and marital fidelity as typically restrictive inventions of the Demiurge, and held orgies in which the free indulgence of every perversion seems to have been mingled with ritual magic: a field in which Gnostic ideas are rife to this day. Yet the primary sources of later Gnosticism, the recently-discovered Nag Hammadi scrolls (hidden in the late fourth century AD), propose a much more sober doctrine based on the highest ethics. While their theology is as radical as any, the reader feels closer to Zen Buddhism than to modern Satanism when confronted with their *koan*-like paradoxes, and instructed by the true God: 'Do not be ignorant of me anywhere or at any time. Be on your guard!' (*Nag Hammadi Library*, p. 271).

51 *Cock and Hen*
Intaglio gem. London, British Museum.

Sex was as important, in a positive way, to certain Gnostic sects as it was, in a negative way, to the contemporary Christian ascetics. It was a means of experiencing the life force and of exhausting it, of propagating universal love, of asserting one's independence from the rules of conventional morality, and eventually of attaining unity with the Concealed God. The sexual magic publicized by Aleister Crowley gives a good impression of the nature and goals of some Gnostics, and his fate indicates some of the dangers involved in such a path, more fully discussed in the Introduction.

While this gem is not explicitly Gnostic, its sexual yet not salacious subject and the choice of the cock suggest a Gnostic origin. Cocks were recognized by all the Near Eastern peoples as sacred to the Sun, whom they greet at dawn. The cock's crow traditionally banishes the evil forces of the night, as for the Barbelognostics the unfettered indulgence of the sexual impulse brings freedom from the constricting laws of the evil Demiurge.

52 *Abraxas*
Bronze statuette. Lausanne, Archaeological Museum.

The name Abraxas or Abrasax is often found in association with an armed figure with the head of a cock and serpents for legs. His identity is uncertain, some maintaining that he is the Supreme Principle and others that he is the same as Jehovah: a confusion not unknown in other religions. In view of the association of Abraxas images and inscriptions with magic, it seems likely that the entity in question is a daemon, of terrifying aspect but not necessarily evil nature, who can be invoked, like the ferocious aspects of certain Oriental gods, for protection. Hence he is often depicted on gemstones suitable for wearing as rings. The form in which he appeared to the inward eye lingered on in folk memory as the cockatrice or basilisk whose glance turns the beholder to stone.

53 *Archontic Funeral Stele*
From Hebron, fourth century A D. Private collection.

Little enough imagery can definitely be identified as Gnostic in origin, and of that only a fraction is properly understood by anyone. Several stelae of this kind were found in Palestine and associated with the Archontic sect of Gnostics. This late sect rejected the official religions and relied on the soul's own powers to traverse the spheres of the manifested universe and reach the Great Mother above. They regarded the rulers of the seven planetary spheres as opponents of mankind, as indeed they are if the goal lies above those spheres (see Introduction). The apparently crude funeral stelae are probably more significant than one might suppose. One recognizes on them allusions to numerical and cosmological doctrines, in the divided circles, crosses and trees. They may be in the nature of spiritual biographies, recording the initiations of the deceased.

54 *Moon Goddess*
Stele from Argos, second or third century A D. London, British Museum.

This effigy of a lunar goddess within the Zodiac belongs with the many other cosmic divinities pictured in this book; but it is associated with Gnosticism on account of an inscription on the underside of the stele:

Ιαια · φραινφιρι · κανωθρα ·
λυκυσυντα · δωδεκακιστη · Σαβαωθ ·
αβωθερσας

These untranslatable words may have been added long after the stele was carved, adapting it to a new and magical purpose. They were of course invisible, facing the ground when the stele is set upright, but that is unimportant. What is significant in magic is the mere fact of their presence: a belief surviving in the topical objects placed beneath foundation stones or in space capsules, destined for the sight of beings we cannot imagine.

Painting on vault of the Mausoleum of the
Aurelii, Rome, first half of the third century
AD.

The Naassene Gnostics had a doctrine of a
Divine Triad comprising the First Man, the
Second Man and the First Woman; and
these three, Jérôme Carcopino suggested,
are figured on the central medallion of this
Christian Gnostic tomb. The First Woman
is Sophia, the Divine Wisdom,
corresponding to what orthodox
Christianity called the Holy Spirit. In the
second circle are four peacocks and four
male figures. The iridescent tails of these
birds relate them to the canopy of the stars,
hence to the hope of immortality in the
perfect realm above the Zodiac. The men
have the attributes of both the first and the
second persons of the Trinity, and hence
represent Christ, who was an emanation
from these, descending to save mankind.
The women in the third zone are human
souls like Sophia awaiting their saviour,
while the hippocamps are the traditional
vehicles for the journey of souls across the
upper waters to the Fortunate Isles. For a
fleeting moment, both Christian and pagan
ideas are held in perfect harmony and
balance.

VIII *Christianity*

The teachings of Jesus are simple and radical: 'Love your enemies'; 'The Kingdom of Heaven is within you'; 'My Father is greater than I'. No one knows, of course, which statements accredited to the Jesus of the Gospels were really spoken by him, so much have they been edited before reaching their canonical state. But when they actually go against official Church dogma or practice, it is safe to say that there is something authentic about them that has miraculously survived censorship. In these three statements, for example, we have an ethical system, a definition of Man, and a clarification of Jesus's own nature, quite at variance with the later teachings of most Christian Churches.

To love one's enemies and to 'turn the other cheek' is what Jesus himself did, and as such it represents the highest practice of the way of Love. Anyone can love themselves, most people can love their neighbours, a few can even extend the term to include the despised 'Samaritan'. But to love your enemies and not to resist their assaults: that is a counsel of perfection, and to follow it a true imitation of Christ. It is the same thing as 'loving God with all thy heart, mind and strength', because it involves perceiving and loving the Divinity within each human being. Who knows how many gallant attempts have been made by insignificant people: how many personal kindnesses, unsung sacrifices, and inner experiences of the love of God? The history books record mainly the unloving side of Christianity: the exclusivity which began with St Peter's rejection of the Gentile faithful, and gathered momentum until by the fourth century the bishops were torturing and executing Arians and other heretic Christians.

If the Kingdom of Heaven is within each human being, then one can seek and find it there, as well as in external institutions and practices. Here again, the mystics generally keep quiet about their experiences, and we do not know how many have found the Kingdom, and the Christ, within. We do know that the Roman Church has said that there is no salvation without its aid, and that the Protestant sects too set themselves up as indispensable bridges, or bastions, between a man and his own divine Spirit.

The third saying of Jesus should have been sufficient to prevent the confusion which is at the very root of official Christianity. The Absolute One; the Demiurge; the Christ; the Overseer of the Jewish people; Jesus of Nazareth: these are five distinct entities on five very different levels of being. A confusion of levels has led to the dogma which tries to unite them, and incidentally to the spilling of much ink and more blood.

At the same time, there has always been an esoteric Christian tradition, usually concealed for fear of exoteric persecution. Some of the Gnostic schools, the Celtic Church, the Cathars and Albigenses, the Fedeli d'Amore and Knights Templar, the Masons, Rosicrucians and Illuminati, and in the Orthodox Church the Hesychasts: these have kept the Light of the World burning – sometimes under a bushel, it is true – and together they form a chain of Christian Mysteries. Modern Theosophists and Anthroposophists claim to hand down the esoteric Christian tradition in their view of the status of Jesus Christ. According to this, Jesus of Nazareth was a man, the son of Mary and Joseph, raised to the highest moral and intellectual standards under the guidance of the Essenes (see Introduction). At the age of thirty, on the occasion of his Baptism, Jesus gave his body and mind to be vehicles on earth for a being of higher order than mankind, indeed one of the highest gods in the hierarchy of this solar system: the Christ. This god worked through Jesus for three years, then at the Crucifixion departed. The physical body of Jesus disappeared from the earth on Easter Day (just as has been observed in modern Tibet in the case of liberated sages). He manifested for a time in his astral body, teaching his closest disciples. The Imitation of Christ, for us humans, is therefore the offering of our bodies and souls so that our own 'Christ', our own divine Spirit, can manifest through them.

56 *Cross with Logos Symbol*
Episcopal throne, early medieval period.
Torcello Cathedral.
Whereas the open hand with all fingers
outstretched is a sign of creation and power,
the hand pointing with two fingers alone
symbolizes thought, logos, and teaching. It
is the hand of Christ as the Word of God,
and here it is given a cosmic context by the
Sun and Moon, placed within a cross that is
Christ's but also the archetypal quaternity
(see Pls 67, 142). Just as Mithras or Jupiter
fills the whole cosmos for their devotees, so
Christ's teaching and his saving Word
dominate the universe for the Christian.

57 *The Trinity at the Creation of Man*
The 'Dogmatic Sarcophagus' from San
Paolo fuori le Mura, Rome, fourth century
AD. Rome, Museo Pio Clementino.

The dogmatic nature of this carving was
probably directed against the Arian belief in
the inequality of the Holy Trinity. The
orthodox view is here given pictorial
expression in that three identical bearded
men, the Father, Son and Holy Spirit,
preside over the Creation, raising Eve from
the recumbent body of Adam. The robed
younger figure who stands between the
fully grown Adam and Eve is, in turn,
identified as the Son, for he appears four
further times elsewhere on the monument,
performing four miracles. The changing of
the water into wine, the multiplication of
the loaves, the raising of Lazarus, and the
restoration of sight to the blind are chosen
to emphasize the creative power of Jesus,
and to support the doctrine that he was not
created by his Father but was present from
the very beginning. He was there in the
Garden of Eden, and witnessed the Fall of
Man which he was to redeem.

The view of Arius holds that before the
worlds were made, the Supreme Father
created out of nothing a Logos, a
subordinate creative and divine Principle;
and that it was this which entered into Jesus
of Nazareth, taking the place of his human
spirit. The Logos is thus a god of a lower
order than the Absolute One (how could it
be otherwise?) and Jesus is its avatar. This
view was debated at the Council of Nicaea
in AD 325, and defeated by the faction
which then became the decreers of
orthodoxy for all of Christendom,
supported by the strong secular arm of the
Emperor Constantine.

58 *St Callixtus*
Gilded glass, fourth century A D. Paris,
Bibliothèque Nationale.

The story of Pope Callixtus gives much
insight into the situation of Christians
around A D 200. Callixtus was a slave who
managed a bank until on accusation from
some Jews he was condemned to the
Sardinian mines. He must already have
made friends in high places, for his release
was procured by one of the Emperor
Commodus' favourite concubines, Marcia,
who was also a Christian. Callixtus rose to
the pontificate and, true to his old
profession, proceeded to lay the foundation
of the Church's wealth by acquiring
property, including the catacombs which
for two centuries were to be the Christians'
cemeteries, chapels, poor-houses and hiding-
places.

59 *Christ's Nativity and the Three Magi*
From a sarcophagus in the Christian
Lapidarium, Arles.

Christ was traditionally born in a cave
where an ox and an ass were stabled. That is
to say, the inner Christ is born in the heart,
where good and evil both dwell. The ass
had long been a symbol of the dark powers,
e.g. of Set, the Egyptian 'Satan', while the
bovine is the true sacrificial beast, the most
useful to mankind and to the earth. Beneath
the nativity scene the three Magi, not yet
shown as kings, notice the star. Their
'Persian' dress of Phrygian caps and trousers
would have suggested that of Mithras, the
Dioscuri, Attis and other Oriental deities;
and perhaps the allusion is deliberate, as they
prepare to kneel before the new-born god.

60 *Christ, the Alpha and Omega*
Ceiling painting, end of the fourth century
AD. Rome, Cemetery of Commodilla:
Cubicle of Leo.

The Christian perspective regards history
not as cyclic but as running in a straight line
from the Creation to Judgment Day. Christ
was present at the beginning as the creative
Word of God (see Pl. 57), and he will be
there at the end as Judge. Hence the Alpha
and Omega which flank him in the
traditional Christian iconography.

61 *Christ, Daniel and the Dragon*
Gilded glass, fourth century A D. London,
British Museum.

Many associations would have sprung up in
the fourth-century mind in response to this
image. According to the story in the
Apocrypha, Daniel undertook to slay
without a weapon the dragon worshipped
by the Babylonians. He poisoned it with
cakes of pitch, outraging its devotees who
had him thrown into the lions' den in which
he remained miraculously unharmed. Christ
does not of course figure in the story, but
here he seems to be Daniel's prompter,
wearing for the first known time a halo.
The choice of this odd subject may be
explainable as a polemic against those
Gnostics who identified Christ with the
dragon or serpent of Eden.

62 *Jonah and the Whale*
Detail of an Alexandrian ivory diptych,
early sixth century A D. Ravenna, Museo
Nazionale.

Jonah, like his putative contemporary
Arion, was thrown overboard by offended
mariners and saved by the intervention of a
sea-monster. The two stories aptly sum up
the difference between the Judaic and
Hellenic attitudes: for while Arion charmed
the dolphin by his music and was carried to
shore singing on the beast's back, Jonah was
trying to run away from the will of the
Lord, and had to spend a most
uncomfortable three days' journey in the
whale's belly. For Christian symbolism the
Prophet is an anticipation of Christ, who
rose from the tomb on the third day, and
hence a symbol of every soul's resurrection.

IX Mithras and Aion

Mithraism was the Freemasonry of the Roman world. Whatever its ancestry in the ancient religion of Persia, it became something very different as soon as it left its native soil and took root in late Republican Rome. Like the other cults of Oriental origin, it moved with the vast commerce in human beings that is such a notable, and tragic, feature of the ancient world. Hundreds of thousands of slaves and soldiers, forcibly transported for life away from their homelands, could carry but one thing with them as they travelled: their faith. The cult of Mithras is one that travelled well, from Syria to Scotland, and it did not matter much that official recognition of it in Rome was comparatively tardy, in the later second century A D. It is futile to try to correlate the widely scattered monuments and inscriptions with the ancient Persian religion, in the hope of coming up with a single Mithraic creed. But the social aspects are easily enough described. The adherents were bound to no exclusive allegiance, being permitted like present-day Masons to belong to any church, or none; but they were bound by secrecy, which they observed (as people always did in ancient times) with a holy dread. Hence our relations with Mithraism will always be determined more by curiosity than by certainty. The Mithraic community was all male: women gravitated to the parallel cult of Cybele or the exclusively female one of Bona Dea. The congregations were small: no surviving Mithraeum could house more than a hundred, but of course bigger lodges may have formed, and dissolved, at army camps. There were no social barriers, so that slaves and privates could become high initiates. The ceremonies were solemnly enacted and the initiations quite awe-inspiring.

Whether Mithraism resembled Masonry further, in being based on the esoteric truths common to all branches of the Perennial Philosophy, is another matter. The divergence of symbolism from one Mithraeum to another is quite startling, and scholars have admitted that the local artisans did not always understand what they were depicting. One can go further and say that in that case they must have lacked proper direction, and that perhaps the masters themselves were none too sure of their symbolism and exactly what it meant.

The very impossibility of fitting the basic Mithraic symbols satisfactorily with those of the esoteric inheritance of mankind suggests that the whole affair may have been an invented religion rather than a revealed one, perhaps on a level with Mormonism which similarly takes as its starting point an ancient and authentic revelation.

When one studies Mithraic symbolism, one is struck by the constant shifting of levels: from the astronomical to the metaphysical, from the psychological to the ontological. Who is the Mithras of the Mysteries? He is one of the gods, lower than Ahura Mazda (the Supreme Deity of Light of the Persians) but higher than the visible Sun. He is creator and orderer of the universe, hence a manifestation of the creative Logos or Word. Seeing mankind afflicted by Ahriman, the cosmic power of darkness, he incarnated on earth. His birth on 25 December was witnessed by shepherds. After many deeds (some of them described with the plates) he held a last supper with his disciples and returned to heaven. At the end of the world he will come again to judge resurrected mankind and after the last battle, victorious over evil, he will lead the chosen ones through a river of fire to blessed immortality. It is possible to prepare oneself for this event during life by devotion to him, and to attain a degree of communion with him through the sacramental means of initiation.

No wonder the early Christians were disturbed by a deity who bore so close a resemblance to their own, and no wonder they considered him a mockery of Christ invented by Satan, their own Dark Lord. In a certain way they may have been right. It is my suspicion – which, unfortunately, cannot be bolstered by scholarly evidence – that Roman Mithraism was born from some clairvoyant sense of the coming of Christ, seen through the perspective of Zoroastrian dualism. It is precisely the connections with Christianity that make Mithraism so interesting, and so confusing. Persian dualism is a faith of the Age of Aries (second–first millennia BC), which is the sign of the Sun's exaltation and Mars' rulership; so Mithras, the solar warrior, is still re-enacting the close of the previous Age of Taurus (fourth–third millennia BC) by slaying the cosmic Bull. All the Arien leaders are fighters: the ram-horned Moses, Ammon and Mars/Ares himself. Jesus Christ, on the other hand, immolates the age of war in the only way possible: by sacrificing himself as the Ram or Lamb of God. In doing so he ushers in the Age of Pisces (second–first millennia AD), the era which cherishes in its heart an ideal of devotion and love.

63 *Egg-birth of Mithras*
Relief from Housesteads Fort,
Northumberland, second century AD.
Newcastle-on-Tyne, Museum of
Antiquities.

In one of his many syncretistic guises,
Mithras springs fully-armed from the
broken halves of the cosmic egg, like Phanes
Protogonus, the first-born god of light in
the Orphic theogony (cf. Pl. 142). The
world-egg represents the entirety, *in
potentia*, of one cosmic cycle, and its
sundering symbolizes the polarity of
positive and negative forces without which
no world could unfold in time and space.
Mithras is both the personified creator who
breaks the egg, and the mediator between
the opposites who eventually heals the rift
and reconciles the warring factions. He is
born in the sign of Capricorn, i.e. at the
winter solstice: the light of the world enters
on the darkest day of the year.

64 *Mithras as Sun God*
Votive stele from Carrawbrough,
Northumberland, second century A D.
Newcastle-on-Tyne, Museum of
Antiquities.

Beyond the mention of his name in the
inscription, 'Deo invicto Mitrae', there is
nothing to distinguish this figure from Sol.
He holds in his right hand a whip to drive
his quadriga, and his rays pierce the stone to
allow the light of a lamp to shine through
from behind. Mithras is sometimes
identified with the Sun, yet sometimes put
in actual opposition to it. According to one
legend he stole the Sun God's cattle,
slaughtered the cosmic Bull, and thus made
possible the generation of mankind. The
myths of cattle-stealing or cattle-herding
gods, such as Hermes and Krishna, allude to
the appropriation by spiritual monads of
human bodies prepared through physical
generation, or in Platonic language to the
vivification of *soma* by *nous*. It is the task of
religions to lead these monads up again to
their proper home.

65 *The Child Mithras turning the Zodiac*
Gallic relief. Trier, Rheinisches
Landesmuseum.

The divine Child holds in his hand the
globe of the earth, just as the Christ Child
in medieval icons holds the royal orb
surmounted by his symbol, the cross. Both
are imagined as lords of a limited,
geocentric cosmos: a manifested physical
universe which extends as far as the eye can
see, i.e. to the stars of the Zodiac, placed
'foursquare' between the winds or
archangels. The beasts below, often shown
in the tauroctones (bull-slaying
monuments), probably represent the
elements and four signs of the Zodiac
connected with generation: Serpent-Fire-
Leo (cf. the shape of the 'Leo' symbol);
Dog-Earth-Virgo (dogs are sacred to
Mercury, ruler of the sign); Raven-Air-
Libra; Scorpion-Water-Scorpio. But
Mithraic iconography is so inconsistent –
the Scorpion is absent here, for example –
that one cannot offer any blanket
explanations of its meaning.

< **66** *Rock-birth of Mithras*
Roman relief. Dublin, Trinity College
Library.

If the egg-birth within the Zodiac
symbolizes the creative action of the
spiritual principle in a limited cosmos, the
rock-birth shows the opposite: the breaking
of the spirit out of the solidity of physical
matter. The struggle of the spirit to free
itself from the adamantine bonds of the
body is a second birth, achieved by the great
avatars and sages during their life, and
performed with more or less difficulty at
every man's death. Birth into one world is
always death to another, and vice versa.

67 *Mithras receiving his Command*
Relief from Dieburg, before A D 260.
Dieburg, Kreismuseum.

The central, seated figure of Zeus-Ahura Mazda is delegating his authority to a cloaked Mithras of the sun-charioteer type. Leroy Campbell (see Bibliography) identifies the four women around the throne as the four Seasons, and the youths leading horses as the four Elements. This is a creative act: the cyclic motion of time, represented by the Seasons, is reflected in the rotation of the Elements. Note that the ages of the Elements and their degrees of motion increase, from the static boy feeding his horse at upper left, round clockwise to the vigorous young man with his trotting steed at lower left. The same archetypal quaternity will be carried down to the foursquare earth, outside the heavenly circle, by the four Winds who blow at the corners. At the bottom of the circle are reclining figures with amphora and cornucopia, and a head of the Oceanus type. One frequently finds this configuration (e.g. Pl. 83) as a symbol of the fruitful Earth, with its rivers and the seas. But here the figures are the immaterial ideas of the world, still held within the charmed circle of the heavenly mind.

68 *Tauroctone*
Relief from Dura Europos, AD 170–1. Yale University, Gallery of Fine Arts.

The central image of Mithraic iconography is his slaying of the cosmic Bull which Ormuzd, god of light, had created, in order to save it from the clutches of Ahriman, god of darkness. The myth can be interpreted on several levels. *Terrestrially* it represents the sun's gift of fertility to crops and creatures: the pouring of vitality into the ground or into the womb from which new life can arise. This is the level explored in Frazer's *The Golden Bough*. *Psychologically* it is the sacrifice or sublimation of the sexual powers, of which the bull is an obvious symbol, in the interests of higher development, as practised by monks and yogis. *Astronomically* it marks the end of the Taurean Age of mankind (fourth-third millennia BC) which preceded the Arien Age (second-first millennia BC) to which the Persian myths belong. *Theologically* it is the action of one of the lower gods, like Jehovah or Jupiter, who 'slay' the archetypal Ideas to create the physical matter without which our world could not exist. (Ahriman, mistakenly called a principle of evil, is only 'dark' because he represents an unknowable, higher level of gods, who have no possible commerce with matter or with the limited time and space signified by the circum-scribing Zodiac.) *Physically* it is the trans-mutation of matter into energy, taking place between the positive and negative potencies. *Metaphysically* it is the encounter between the infinite cosmic substance (Taurus) and the binding cosmic idea (Gemini).

69 *Tauroctone*
Relief from Heddernheim. Wiesbaden,
Städtisches Museum.

Just like the Crucifixion, the Mithraic
sacrifice takes place between Sun and Moon
and under the eye of the Father God
(Jupiter, in the preceding plate). The good
and bad thieves also have their
correspondences in the two torch-bearers
Cautes and Cautopates, who have as many
meanings as the sacrifice itself. They are at
every level reflections of the primal duality
of light and darkness, life and death, spirit
and matter, etc. Cautopates, with lowered
torch, rules the autumn equinox and winter
solstice, the barren half of the year; Cautes,
with raised torch, is the return of fertility in
spring and summer. But in southern Iranian
reliefs their symbolism is reversed, because
there the scorching summer sun withers the
vegetation which flourishes in the cooler,
wetter months. Much of Mithraic
iconography seems to belong in the
venerable tradition of vegetation
symbolism. But to those versed in the
Hermetic-Platonic tradition, Cautopates also
signifies the extinction of the soul's light on
its entry into the body, and Cautes its
rebirth after 'death'. This relief, so rich in
imagery, includes also the solar and lunar
chariots, Mithras' capture of the cosmic Bull
and his reconciliation with Sol, and the four
beasts. Leroy Campbell has made the most
thorough investigation of the iconography,
but even his results are inconclusive.

70 Sol with Raven
Wall-painting in the Capua Mithraeum,
third century A D.

In this detail from a painted tauroctone, Sol
is both personifier of the positive pole,
balanced by negative Luna on the opposite
side, and of Mithras' father and director
Ormuzd with his messenger-bird the raven.
A major philosophical difficulty is involved
here. On the one hand Mithras is the
mediator between the cosmic opposites
Ormuzd and Ahriman (superficially called
good and evil), and as such he reconciles this
ethical split in the psyche of mankind. On
the other hand, he takes sides with the good
against the evil, thus exacerbating the
conflict. How can they both be true? The
further East one goes, the better this seems
to be understood. Vedantists and Buddhists
know that, on the earthly level, evil
certainly exists and must be fought. But it
has no metaphysical reality, and a higher
standpoint shows it as merely the mirror
image of an equally unreal 'good'.

71 Mithraic Magus
Wall-painting in the Dura Europos
Mithraeum, third century A D.

The nudity of Greek gods and of the Greeks
themselves was repugnant to the people of
the Middle East, whose fear of their own
sexuality led even before the Muslims to
excesses such as the veiling of women. This
overdressed Magus, and indeed Mithras
himself in his cloak and trousers, must have
seemed as exotic to the Graeco-Roman
world as the Japanese in kimonos did to
nineteenth-century Europe. One garment,
the 'Phrygian' cap, became a universal
symbol of the Oriental cults, being worn by
Mithras, Attis, the Kabeiroi, the Dioscuri,
and their servitors. Later it became the
headgear of medieval Masons, the *sans-
culottes*, and La Liberté herself. Its
symbolism is one of supreme spiritual
attainment, represented also in Osiris' white
crown, Buddha's topknot, Shou-hsing's
swollen cranium, and the tiaras of Shiva and
the Pope.

72 *Aion with Keys*
Statue from Sidon, fourth century A D.
Private collection, Paris.

The imposing effigy of the leontocephalic
god is often found in proximity to Mithraic
monuments, and to him has been given the
designation of Aion: the boundless 'Time'
which presides unmoved and unmoving over
the entire universe. His keys unlock the two
solsticial gates. The silver one is to the Gate
of Cancer which leads to the Way of the
Ancestors (Pitri-yana) and to reincarnation.
The golden one is to the Gate of Capricorn,
the Way of the Gods (Deva-yana) which
leads beyond the Circle of Necessity, i.e. to
release from the round of birth and death.
These are the two routes through which the

soul can exit from the world at death, and
the Capricorn gate is the one through which
the gods descend to earth, Mithras as well as
Christ being born at the winter solstice.
Buddhists would probably identify Aion
with Shin-je, Judge of the Dead, the
monstrous figure who turns the wheel of
the six worlds.

73 *Aion with Apron*
Statue from the Villa Albani, late first
century A D. Vatican Museum.

Aion's four wings and serpent represent
time with its fourfold divisions and cyclic
motion. With his open lion's mouth he
devours his progeny at the end of each cycle

of cosmic manifestation. Like Shiva, another supreme god of cyclic creation and destruction, Aion here has four arms, though what the front ones held we do not know: probably sceptre and keys. The back pair clutch arrows carved onto the wings. The accompanying symbols here are definitely chthonic: three-headed Cerberus, the guard-dog of the underworld, and a mass of snakes. To an ordinary Mithraist the conception of Aion as a god of Hades like Pluto or Serapis was probably more familiar than the lofty explanations of Orphism. The lions' heads would denote courage, and the eye on the breast intelligence – though it is of course the 'eye of the heart' through which the soul knows truth. The apron, an Egyptian garment later adopted by Freemasonry, may serve to emphasize the purity to which devotees of Mithras aspired. This figure, in fact, may well represent the attitude with which a Mithraist hopes to approach, and transcend, the world of shades.

74   *Aion on Globe*
Relief from the Villa Albani, period of Commodus (AD 180–93). Rome, Museo Torlonia.

Unlike the cosmic gods who are shown inside the Zodiac, Aion stands above a Zodiac-encircled globe or wears the signs on his body. Here the signs are indicated by the twelve divisions of his sceptre. The two bands crossing the globe recall the World Soul's method of creation in Plato's *Timaeus*, by crossing the two circles of world-stuff in the form of an **X**. Aion is a creator, but not of worlds: he emanates metaphysical principles or gods. In the Persian theogony he is Zervan, whose two sons are the opposites Ormuzd and Ahriman between which Mithras mediates. So he is in a way the highest aspect of Mithras, being beyond rather than between the opposites.

X *Cybele and Attis*

The Great Mother Goddess has seldom lacked devotees. In every culture of mankind she appears, sometimes loving and nurturing, at other times devouring and destroying. In her first aspect, personified by goddesses like Isis, Hera, Fricka and Mary, she protects women (especially in childbirth, being herself a mother), maintains the proprieties of marriage and the family, and rules the hearth and home. She is a never-failing source of comfort to whom one appeals for help as one did, as a child, to one's own mother. The Romans knew this archetype in their indigenous goddess Juno, the wife of Jupiter, but the feminine was never very strong in the State religion, dominated as it was by warrior gods and national heroes. The other aspect of the Goddess concerns the unknown, the mysterious and magical, of which women have a greater intuitive understanding than men. While the extroverted gods are at work in the world, the Great Mother stays at home and rules in the interior realm of the unconscious. Here she is Luna, Astarte, Hecate, Kali: the goddess of nocturnal rites and orgiastic plummetings into the abyss of the subconscious. It is this aspect that official Roman religion, and Roman life, seem to have lacked. The dour, masculine character of Republican Rome needed a counterbalance, an escape valve for aspirations which the State religion ignored. So when in 204 BC, on the advice of the Delphic Oracle, the Romans fetched the Great Mother from Pessinus (near modern Sivrihisar in central Turkey), their act had a psychological rightness, involving an acceptance of irrational and uncontrollable forces.

Cybele's homeland was Anatolia, a land for which the Romans had a sentimental attachment since it was thence, after the Trojan War, that Aeneas had sailed with his Trojan heroes to found the City of Rome. Cybele took shape there as a black stone the size of a fist, probably a meteorite, set as the face of a silver statue. What the Pessinians felt about surrendering their cultic image we do not know, but Cybele was duly installed in a temple on the Palatine Hill and worshipped there for over five hundred years.

Of the several legends concerning Attis, the standard one in the Imperial period tells that he was a Phrygian shepherd of unusual comeliness who was beloved of the Mother of the Gods. It is doubtful that their love was ever consummated, which is probably why Attis fell in love with a nymph, traditional prey of classical shepherds. The Mother was so incensed by his infidelity that she caused him to become insane, in which condition he castrated himself and died. After death he was reborn and reunited with her. Cybele and Attis are worshipped as a pair, but they are not equals like Jupiter and Juno, or Isis and Osiris: Attis is deified, but remains definitely secondary to his mother, just as in the Arian view Jesus is not the equal of God the Father. And if generations of Christians believed that Jesus died on the cross as the only means to pacify his father's anger at mankind, it was no more absurd for the devotees of Attis and Cybele to worship a jealous goddess and her mutilated son.

The parallels, as in the case of Mithraism, are worth pursuing further. The most solemn ritual of Cybele's worship, if we can judge from the evidence of numerous inscriptions, was the *taurobolium*, or bull-sacrifice. The bull was slaughtered on a perforated platform, through which the blood poured down to bathe the initiate standing in a pit beneath. One could celebrate a taurobolium, like a Mass, either for one's own benefit or for that of another, especially the Emperor. Afterwards the devotee was considered in some sense 'born again'. Poorer people made do with a *criobolium*, in which a ram was killed, and were 'washed in the blood of the Lamb'. Both Mithraism and Christianity seem to have sublimated this crudely physical rite: the Mithraists by placing the icon of the tauroctonous Mithras in the place of honour in their sanctuaries, but not actually performing the slaughter there, and the Christians by drinking their saviour's blood in the form of sacramental wine.

The precise relation of the taurobolium to Cybele's worship is unknown, since her dogmas and liturgies are lost. But she was certainly a goddess who demanded sacrifice, and the taurobolium was probably a vicarious substitute for the shedding of human blood. For some of her devotees, however, this was not sufficient. In her native Orient, the most fervent of them would pledge eternal fealty to her by following the example of Attis and emasculating themselves. Thereafter they were totally devoted to her service, assuming the role of mendicant ascetics and the name of Galli ('Cocks'). The Romans reacted with a mixture of fascination and horror to these unmanned hierophants, who, at least in the West, affected extravagant costumes, make-up and jewellery. History was to repeat itself in the seventeenth and eighteenth centuries, when Rome was again full of idolized and effeminate *castrati*, their manhood sacrificed not to religion but to Art.

The great festival of Cybele and Attis took place around the vernal equinox. In the middle of the fourth century AD, presumably following ancient tradition, the spring rites would begin on 15 March with the entry of the 'reed-bearers', whose exact significance is uncertain. A week later, at the equinox proper, was the 'entry of the tree', the evergreen pine under which Attis died and which was revered and mourned as a symbol of the god himself. It is impossible to ignore the associations with Jesus' entry into Jerusalem surrounded by palm-bearers, and his bearing of the cross or tree which became his chief symbol. And this is not all: on 22 March the tree, decked with funereal purple, was laid to rest in the temple of the Mother as in a sepulchre. The next day was one of vociferous mourning, and on the day following, the 'day of blood', the Mother's worshippers would whip themselves and some of them, carried away by ecstasy, would perform the irreversible act. With the dawn of 25 March came the day of rejoicing for some – convalescence for others – as Attis' resurrection was celebrated.

Not long after, on 4 April, fell the commemoration of Cybele's entry into Rome, and on 10 April the anniversary of the dedication of her temple on the Palatine. These feasts of the Mother, marked by banquets, games and dramas, were the contribution of the Roman aristocrats, in contrast to the fanatic and essentially foreign Attis-rites of March. The two groups of festivals reflect the dual aspects of Cybele mentioned above: on the one hand the all-demanding and devouring mistress; on the other, the benign giver of life and the fruits of the earth. Again we can see the two options open to the spiritual aspirant, the way of denial and the way of acceptance.

75 *Cybele in the Zodiac*
Relief from Transjordan, early second
century A D. Cincinnati, Art Museum, and
private collection, Amman.

Nelson Glueck made the happy discovery
that these two fragments belong to a single
sculpture of a Victory supporting a goddess
in the Zodiac. Cybele-Tyche-Atargatis
assumes a rôle like that of Jupiter in Pl. 2,
representing the power that fills the visible
universe. This power can be imagined
female, just as well as male, and the races of
man have worshipped it in both guises,
depending on their prejudices and social
structure. The most primitive cultures
known to anthropologists seem to be
matriarchal; later ones are patriarchal, and
their supreme god changes sex accordingly.

76 *Cybele riding a Lion*
Roman coin, second century AD. London,
British Museum.

The two great goddesses of the Zodiac are
the Mother, whose sign is Cancer, and the
Virgin, whose sign is Virgo. Of course
Cybele's domination over the king of beasts
is an evocative image of her strength, but
the astrological symbolism goes further than
that. As Virgo follows Leo in the Zodiac, so
the power of the universe represented by
the Lion is harnessed and tamed by the
Virgin goddess of Nature, who in turn gives
birth to all living creatures.

77 *Mother Goddess with Twins*
Terracotta, *c.* AD 300. London, British
Museum.

Terracotta statuettes such as this one were
mass-produced in the ancient world, like
popular Roman Catholic art today, as
votive objects for the home. In this
particular case, even the image has remained
unchanged through the millennia: and no
wonder, for as long as there are mothers and
children, with all their attendant concerns,
so long will devotion to the Great Mother
Goddess continue, whether she is called Isis,
Astarte, Cybele or Mary. The projection of
human motherhood onto a goddess is
logically absurd, yet these archaic beliefs
hold a symbolic truth far stronger than the
shallow rationalism that tries to demolish
them: they conceal an intuition of a living
universe of beings in which each has others
under its care. No one is alone, no creature
is totally abandoned or forgotten by their
higher principles which have the task of
vivifying, nurturing and eventually
weaning them, so that they can become
'mothers' in their turn.

78 *Procession in Honour of Cybele*
Wall-painting in the Via dell' Abbondanza,
Pompeii, *c.* first century A D.

In the annual celebration of Cybele's entry
into Rome, the life-sized image of the
goddess was placed on a litter and attended
by worshippers with musical instruments
and libation bowls. Processions in which the
deity is carried along a prescribed route are
a universal element of religions. Their
arcane purpose is connected with the occult
properties of the earth itself, and with
reinforcing the telluric currents that affect
those who live near them. A procession,
traditionally interspersed with stations (of
which one is depicted here), traces the route
of the currents and, by carrying over them
an image or other object charged with
spiritual power, serves to fix and sanctify
them and to benefit the people taking part
in the rite. In medieval Christianity the
Corpus Christi Day procession was the
principal ritual of this kind, in which the
consecrated Host was carried around the
town. The processions at coronations and
the funeral cortège of a celebrity, still
practised today, serve similarly to distribute
the virtue of the monarch or hero among
his people.

79 *Pensive Attis*
Wall-painting in the House of Pinarius Cerealis, Pompeii, first century AD.

Cupid runs away in horror as Attis contemplates the knife with which he intends to castrate himself. His languid position with crossed legs, also found in the Mithraic supporter Cautopates, may refer to the 'crucifixion' of physical existence from which Attis will soon be free. The sickle-shaped knife is a reminder that Cybele, among her other powers, is a moon goddess, whose wrath can drive men to lunatic actions. This particular representation probably depicts a scene from a stage-play, for the tale of Attis and Cybele was a favourite subject for drama. One can imagine the lost Soliloquy of Attis as he weighs the consequences of his deed.

80 *Dying Attis*
Relief from Glanum, second century BC. St Rémy-de-Provence, Museum.

Attis is here shown dying as he lies contortedly between cypress and palm trees on the banks of the river Gallos. His Pan-pipes and other instruments hang silent, and his cloak billows up as he clutches at his wound. Like Christ on Golgotha, he might well say 'My Goddess, why hast thou forsaken me?' Yet this darkest moment will be succeeded by resurrection and reunion with his parent-lover.

81 *Transfigured Attis*
Statue from Ostia, second century AD. Vatican, Museo Laterano.

The previous plate showed the agonizing aspect of Attis' deed; this shows him serene and kingly, released from worldly pleasures and their attendant miseries. From his head shine solar rays. The river Gallos, now not a seductive nymph but a wise old river god, supports his elbow. Attis' swelling abdomen and soft face are like a woman's: he has become an androgyne, above and beyond sex.

82 *Dancing Attis*
Bronze statuette. Paris, Louvre.

Although there is nothing in the literary
sources to explain this favourite Attis figure
– the young boy, sometimes winged like
Eros, dancing and triumphant – its meaning
is plain. His Phrygian garments, left
unbuttoned from thighs to belly, starkly
emphasize his unmutilated condition. He
who was castrated and died is now reborn,
whole and healed, as a being for whom
sexuality is no longer (or not yet) a source
of suffering. The winged boy symbolizes
the soul of the reborn devotee, free to dance
before the gods in spiritual ecstasy and holy
love. Having 'become as a little child', he
inherits the kingdom of heaven.

83 *Ascension of Attis and Cybele*
Silver dish from Parabiago, fourth century
AD. Milan, Castello Sforzesco.

This magnificent silver charger celebrates
the ascension of the Great Mother with her
son-lover. The key to its meaning is given
by the Emperor Julian in his Oration to the
Mother of the Gods. Attis, he says, is the
lowest of the actual 'gods', being the direct
creator of our earth. (The higher gods create
on ideal planes, above the material one.) At
the bottom of the plate we can see his
work: rivers, ocean, fruitful Tellus and the
Seasons. The earth is good, yet lest Attis'
powers be totally dispersed in working with
matter, he is recalled by his Mother. The
myth tells that he was 'betrayed by a lion',
i.e. by the ether, mediating element
between matter and spirit, and castrated, i.e.
deprived of his lower creative faculties.

Attis, released from his work, gazes
ecstatically at his bride as their lion-drawn
quadriga bears them aloft, surrounded by
dancing Corybantes clashing their swords
against their shields. The Corybantes are the
highest forces below the gods, and
traditional protectors of youthful gods, i.e.
the daemonic or angelic beings who channel
the creative forces into the world. Attis and
Cybele ascend towards the heavens,

represented in the upper zone as the chariots of the Sun and Moon, with the Morning and Evening Stars.

A clue to the esoteric meaning of the picture is found on the right where Atlas sinks, bearing aloft the Genius of a *novus ordo seclorum*, a new cycle succeeding Atlantis. This was one of the Mystery teachings of which Plato was permitted to reveal a fragment; it seems that he knew of the periodic creation and destruction of civilizations, aptly symbolized by Attis' creative work and the periodic withdrawal of his powers. At the end of a cycle everything returns to the great maternal ocean. The alternate solidification and dissolution of worlds is an eternal cycle, though not a pointless one like the Stoics' and Nietzsche's 'eternal recurrence'. It has a direction, and that is why the Serpent of Time, on the extreme right of the plate, winds around a pointed obelisk.

XI *Isis and Serapis*

Egypt held a powerful attraction for the Romans, very much like the fascination which the Orient has exerted more recently on the Western world. Egypt was a place of unfathomable antiquity and strange mores, a land of exotic landscapes whose inhabitants performed inexplicable rituals. A fashion for Egyptianizing motifs and ambience gripped the wealthy Romans of the early Empire like the *chinoiserie* craze of the eighteenth century. The Munich pagoda or the Japanese garden at Woburn Abbey are parallels to Hadrian's Euripus, the miniature Nile landscape with a Serapeum set in the Emperor's pleasure-garden at Tivoli. In religion, too, the alien cultures have infiltrated the modern West, though it has taken longer for Europe and America to have their own Buddhist temples and ashrams. In the case of Rome, the religion came first, travelling as always in the ancient world with the traffic in goods and slaves. Isis was being worshipped in the Piraeus, the port of Athens, by the fourth century BC. By the second century BC she had Roman worshippers too on the holy island of Delos, now a great centre of the slave trade. She crept up to Rome through Magna Graecia, leaving impressive memorials, for instance, at Herculaneum and Pompeii, and by the time of Julius Caesar she and Serapis had a temple and an altar on the Capitoline Hill. Apart from some temporary setbacks, the Egyptian cult was to last in Rome for four centuries, from the reign of Augustus to that of Julian, and enjoy immense prestige and imperial patronage.

Isis was the perfect goddess for this time and place, because she came already wearing an aura of syncretism and universality. In an Egyptian hymn of the first century BC she is addressed thus:

> All mortals dwelling on the infinite earth,
> Thracians and Greeks, even barbarians,
> Pronounce thy blessed name, honoured by all,
> Each in his own tongue and in his own land.
> The Syrians address thee as Astarte,
> Or as Nanaia, or as Artemis.
> Thy subjects of Lycia call thee Leto;

The men of Thrace: 'Great Mother of the Gods'.
In Greece they call thee Hera throned on high,
Or Aphrodite, or well-wishing Hestia,
Rhea or Demeter too. But the Egyptians
Give thee the name Thioui, for thou art,
And thou alone, all of the goddesses
Which divers people call by divers names.

> (First Hymn of Isidoros, from the small
> sanctuary of Madinet Madi in the Fayoum)

Isis is a personification of the same archetype as Cybele, the Great Mother: she is all things feminine, from the first unformed matter of the universe down to the cows which are sacred to her. But she had an advantage over the Anatolian and Syrian goddess in that she came from a civilization with thousands of years of profound religious knowledge behind it. Egyptian religion was admittedly in a state of decline as early as the fourth dynasty, when the Pharaoh Cheops usurped an antediluvian Mystery temple for his own tomb. But even in the fourth century A D the hierophants of Egypt still held the keys to other worlds, and to judge from Apuleius and Iamblichus they were able to unlock the door for suitable candidates, taking them through the death experience (the 'gates of Proserpine') and giving them an unforgettable glimpse of spiritual entities.

Isis and Osiris, according to Plutarch, were originally daemons who were promoted to the order of gods. Even in the higher worlds there is continual evolution and migration, though time, death and individuality are not such as we know them on earth. The usual myth of Isis and her brother-husband places them as sovereigns of pre-dynastic Egypt; and there is no incompatibility between the two accounts. This, in fact, is precisely the reason for the success of Isis, and for the great devotion paid to her for so long. Like Jesus and Mary, she and Osiris were incarnated as humans and suffered all the vicissitudes of human life, before ascending to their own realm. Hence the warm and passionate identification felt by Isiacs and Christians alike. One cannot say the same of Mithras or Attis: there is something coldly theological about them. And as for Cybele, compare her treatment of Attis with Isis' treatment of Osiris. Far from jealously encouraging his mutilation, Isis sought and reassembled the scattered pieces of his body; and when she could not find the phallus, she made him an artificial one with which she conceived their son Horus.

And what of Serapis, that mysterious and little-understood god who arrives on the scene with the foundation of Alexandria? He seems to be a conflation of Zeus, Pluto and Asklepios, and he rules as supreme Lord with Isis, though his precise relationship to her, marital or otherwise, is not clear since no myths are told of them. Scholars think him an invention of King Ptolemy Soter, who claims to have been instructed in a dream to find the image of this god. They say that Serapis was a personification of the Apis Bull, an animal avatar of Osiris worshipped at Memphis, the former capital of Egypt, and that Ptolemy, when he established his new capital city, redesigned the god in human form in order to make the Egyptian religion more palatable to Alexandrian Greeks, thus uniting the races under his rule. To leave it at that betokens a cynical view of the gods and their origin, which in the case of Serapis is belied by his obvious power and the devotion he inspired in his worshippers throughout the Graeco-Roman-Egyptian world. He was the presiding deity of Alexandrian civilization, and of all that that city gave to the world, just as Ammon was the god of Thebes, Athena of Athens, Hagia Sophia of Byzantium, and Wotan of the Third Reich. These 'overseers' are just as real as the cultures over which they preside, and they are 'invented' only in the original and literal sense of the word: they are discovered when the time is ripe.

84   *Isis Pelagia*
Fragment from a lamp, second century AD. Delos, Museum.

Isis has many connections with water and those who sail upon it. As a feminine goddess (and a moon goddess at that) she rules the element with all its manifold symbolism. The spring festival, Navigium Isidis, was celebrated on 5 March, invoking her blessing as navigation was resumed after the winter, and ensuring the safe arrival of the Egyptian corn that fed Rome. One of the principal rituals of the festival was the procession of her ship, described in vivid detail by Apuleius. But ships do not only carry corn: they bear souls across the river of death to Paradise. May Isis rather than Charon be our pilot!

85   *Priestess of Isis*
Statue from Hadrian's Villa, second century AD. Rome, Capitoline Museum.

This could equally well be a statue of Isis herself, for the priestess in her ritual clothing and gestures imitates and in a certain sense incarnates the goddess for the worshippers. The sistrum which she brandishes in her right hand is the most characteristic of Isis' attributes. All creative divinities can appropriately be furnished with musical instruments, since all vibrations, including sound, are powerful creative forces. Thus Pan and Attis have their shepherd's pipes, the Mother her tambourine and cymbal, Apollo his lyre, all representing different levels of creative activity. The form of the Isiac sistrum is that of a temenos or sacred enclosure in which the four bars rattle around, representing the interplay of the four elements, their alchemical rotation, and the vibratory forces that organize them into the world we know. All this is under Isis' rule, in her aspect as Mother Nature. In her left hand – the hand of passivity – she holds a pitcher for milk, used in the ceremonies to symbolize Nature's spontaneous nurturing of her creatures. In some of her rites the place of the vessel was taken by a golden model of a breast.

86 Isis Fortuna
Silver statuette from Macon. London, British Museum.

Isis-Fortuna is recognizable by her solar-feather crown, and holds a spilling cornucopia and the rudder with which she steers the course of one's life. (Again active and passive functions are allotted to the right and left hands.) The Stoics declined to believe in Fortuna, rejecting the attitude of the masses who believed that such a goddess, if properly courted, might send undeserved good luck. Of course, that is an unphilosophical view, but there is another way of interpreting this ever-popular figure: as the law of each person's destiny, which may at any time produce unforeseen changes. She is in this interpretation the *karma* of a person, city or state. Thus Plutarch could say that Tyche (as he called her) had abandoned the Assyrians and Persians and moved to the Palatine. To identify her with Isis is to entrust one's fate to the will of the goddess: 'Thy will, not mine, be done.'

87 Isis, Harpocrates and Anubis
Terracotta, probably from Fayoum, found in Campania, second century A D. London, British Museum.

Isis is a model of wifely fidelity, ever devoted to Osiris despite his adultery with her sister Nephthys from which Anubis was born. This jackal-headed or cynocephalus god is charged with the care of the soul during its posthumous journey, and in Egypt this made him the patron of mummification and the other manipulations of the physical body which can speed or retard the soul's progress. Harpocrates is the Graeco-Egyptian name for Horus, Isis' own son, who puts his finger to his lips in a gesture that overtly signifies his infancy but covertly enjoins silence on those who understand him. As the son of Osiris he is a symbol of the soul, reborn like the child Attis (Pl. 82) in its purified state. His cornucopia is a sign of spiritual fullness and completion. Perhaps one can see here a parallel to the popular Christian group of the Virgin and her divine child Jesus with his cousin John the Baptist, his forerunner who in the Baptism bestowed on him his godhead.

88 *Serapis in Majesty*

Statuette, second century A D. London, British Museum.

The features of the early Serapis statues, based on Bryaxis' original of the fourth century B C, most resemble those of Zeus, and the identification is emphasized here by the attendant eagle. But Serapis is clothed like Pluto, and on his right is Cerberus, the three-headed guard-dog of Hades. Like Asklepios he is also a god of healing and oneiromantic revelation: the Serapeum of Alexandria was a centre for incubation and other occult therapies. But most of all Serapis epitomizes that meeting-point of Greece and Egypt which was to be the new spiritual centre of the ancient world, as Rome was its political centre.

89 *Head of Serapis*

Statue, after A D 100. London, British Museum.

Around the second century A D the features of Serapis' statues undergo a slight change, softening almost into androgyny and acquiring forelocks – a hairstyle which several Roman emperors were to imitate (e.g. Pl. 24). On the god's head is his characteristic attribute, the modius (basket) which is said to indicate fertility but actually corresponds to the opening of the highest centre in the body. Yogic authorities might be able to explain the difference between the open basket of Serapis and the closed Phrygian caps of the Oriental deities discussed in Chapter IX. By this time Serapis was 'solarized' and assimilated to all the other sun gods; a similar head was found in the Walbrook Mithraeum, London, whose members evidently accepted both the Persian and the Egyptian god.

90, 91 *Isiac Ceremonies*
Wall-paintings from Pompeii, *c.* first
century AD. Naples, National Museum.

The participation of the laity in religious
services was largely restricted to the outside
of temples, Egyptian and Greek alike. It was
partly the climate that encouraged this, but
it served also to emphasize the division
between exoteric and esoteric rites.
Moreover, the actual building was
conceived of as an architectural incarnation
of the god, so was itself an object worthy of
reverence. Residues of this survive in the
medieval cathedral, which is constructed as
an image of the Divine Man, and in which a
screen separated the laity in the nave from
the collegiate members in the chancel and
sanctuary. These scenes of sacrifice both take
place before the temple steps. In the first, a
mixed choir is ranged on either side (just as
in a cathedral), and the priest descends

towards the altar with an offering. Isis'
sacrifices, like Christ's, never involved the
taking of animal life: milk, honey or herbs
were the chosen elements. The second scene
shows the temple doors acting as the
proscenium arch for a sacred dance or
drama. Both have Egyptian décor,
including imported ibises, the birds of
Thoth who, legend tells, would die of grief
if transported from their native soil.

Another legend attributes to this bird the
habit of giving itself an enema with its long
beak, which is why it symbolizes medicine
and the healing arts in general. The
ceremonies are accompanied musically by
players of the double aulos, which would
sound rather like a bagpipe, and the tinkling
of sistrums. Perhaps a large congregation
should be imagined in the spectator's
position.

92 *Temple Ritual by the Nile*
Part of the Barberini Mosaic, from the
Temple of Fortuna in Palestrina, first
century B C. Rome, National Museum.

Egyptian temple rituals were carried out
uninterruptedly for at least four thousand
years. While changes did occur from time
to time, it seems that the basic practices, like
the use of hieroglyphs and the architectural
and sculptural techniques, were already well
established at what we call the beginning of
Egyptian civilization, i.e. in pre-dynastic
times. No period of slow development has
been identified by archaeologists, who are
thus faced with the awkward question of
how a civilization in its infancy managed to
build monuments such as those at Gizeh and
Saqqara. In fact Egyptian religion was an
inheritance from a previous cycle of
civilization, in which the magical qualities
of images and music (depicted in use here)
were more readily perceived and more
generally understood.

93 *Female Sphinx with Victim*
Funerary monument, first century A D.
Colchester and Essex Museum.

There are two kinds of sphinxes. This is the
later species, of which a specimen terrorized
Thebes until vanquished by Oedipus: she is
Greek, feminine and deadly. Her close
relations are the Sirens, bird-bodied women
who also lure men to their doom and gloat
over their remains. They belong to the
company of semi-human creatures which
may be looked on as elementals, as early
states of the human race, or as
personifications of psychic contents.

94 *Royal Sphinx and Bes*
Votive stele. First century A D or later.
Munich, Glyptothek.

The more ancient Egyptian sphinx is
bearded and crowned, and symbolizes the
completed state of the human being. He has
a man's head, a lion's body, eagle's wings
and a serpent for a tail, thus combining four
elements, four species and four symbolic
functions. On his forehead is the winged
disc of the Sun (also seen separately at the
top), showing his connection to the source
of light, life and inner illumination. The
gnome-like figure of Bes seems out of place
among the svelte bodies of most Egyptian
gods. His origin is Nubian and his appeal
popular: he is a god of sorcery and good
luck, like a genie of the *Arabian Nights*. He
seems to have been a favourite motif for
amulets, invoked to help in childbirth and
against evil spirits, and his oracle at Abydos
flourished until the fourth century A D when
it was suppressed by Constantine II.

95 The 'Tazza Farnese'
Sardonyx cameo, Alexandrian, c. 175 BC.
Naples, National Museum.

There have been many attempts to explain
the imagery of this famous gem, and no
doubt all of them, and more, are applicable.
Its surface reference is to the myth of Osiris,
whose death caused the Nile to flood and
thus to fertilize the land of Egypt. The
Sphinx represents the dead god-king, on
whose back sits Isis. The younger man
above her is Horus, holding a plough-
handle, and the older, seated one with the
cornucopia is Father Nile himself. Attendant
spirits of Winds and Seasons preside over
this vegetation allegory. But in the political
context of its time, Osiris represents the
deified Pharaoh Ptolemy V Epiphanes (to
whom the Rosetta Stone was dedicated)
who died in 181 BC, and his son Ptolemy VI
Philometor who ruled under his mother's
regency. The image is propaganda for the
young king, shown as saviour of his
country.

An astronomical meaning, moreover, is
suggested by Merkelbach, who notices that
the personages are grouped like the
constellations associated with the Nile flood.
Horus is Orion, Isis Sirius, the two flying
Winds Gemini, the nymphs are the Hyades
and Pleiades, whose setting signifies the time
for ploughing and who rise again at harvest
time. The seated figure is Serapis
representing (as a solar god) Leo, the sign
which the Sun enters at flood-time. The
sphinx is the river itself, which begins to rise
on 19 July when Sirius first appears.

**96 Portrait of the Deceased with Anubis and
Osiris**
Painted cloth shroud, c. AD 175–200.
Moscow, Pushkin Museum.

On the left of this sensitive young man is
the effigy of the mummified Osiris, holding
the royal crook and flail, to whom he will
be assimilated when Anubis has done his
work. The jackal god leads him with a
kindly gesture, as he prepares to usher his
soul into the presence of the Judge of the
Dead. There he will read from the scroll he
holds in his hands the story of his life, and
make his statement of justification as he has
learnt it from the Book of the Dead. The
Egyptians, like the Tibetans, were expert in
posthumous matters and procedures, though
the extensive practice of mummification in
later dynastic times denotes a lack of understanding of its true purpose, which was to
prevent the transmigration of highly-
evolved souls so that their conscious
influence might continue on earth.

XII *Dionysus*

The cult of Dionysus had its origins in Thrace, and its temples throughout classical Greece. When the other Greek gods were adapted by the Romans, Dionysus changed his name (to Bacchus) but not his nature. His cult spread with the Empire all round the Mediterranean, and his Mysteries rivalled in prestige those of Demeter at Eleusis. But while the Eleusinian Mysteries were initiations through 'beholding' (*epopteia*), Dionysus' were initiations through action.

Of all the Mystery gods, it is Dionysus whose character has become most firmly fixed in the collective imagination. His worship spells orgies and drunkenness; he personifies the irrational and uncontrollable urges of man and beast; he drives to frenzy the maenads and the poets. His is the dynamic energy which can so easily unmake what his brother Apollo has constructed with such loving care – and the relationship between them, the systole and diastole of cyclic manifestation, is what makes the worlds go round. Modern scholars, devotees by profession of Apollo, tend to blame the excesses of Dionysus' cult on wine, opium, ivy- or toadstool-eating, or on some primitive state of mystic participation which, thankfully, it is impossible for them to recapture. But all their efforts to understand him are vain, for he is innately hostile to rational thought. He cannot be understood, only appreciated; and the late C. Kerényi, with his psychological insight and imagination, knew best how to do this while keeping within the bounds of scholarship. Kerényi subtitled his book on Dionysus 'Archetypal Image of Indestructible Life', finding that the Dionysian cult, from its origins in the depths of archaic Greek culture, furnished intimate contact with the very wellsprings of *zoë*, life, and its counterpart, death.

The myth of Dionysus' origins tells that he was born first from the union of Zeus with Persephone. Zeus designated this Dionysus 'Zagreus' as his heir, but the jealous Titans lured him away while yet a child, dismembered him and devoured all the pieces except for the heart, which Athena rescued and preserved. Zeus in anger reduced the Titans to ashes, from which the new race of mankind was fashioned. Thus each man contains a fragment of Dionysus within his 'titanic' earthly body. From the heart of the god was brewed a love-potion given to Semele, a mortal, who forced her lover – Zeus again – into revealing himself to her in his primal form. The epiphany was so overwhelming as to annihilate her, but the child she was carrying was saved. Zeus enclosed it in his loins until the time came for its birth as the second Dionysus. The young god grew up in Thrace, suckled by goats and raised by satyrs and sileni. When he reached maturity he descended through the Alcyonian Lake to rescue the shade of his mother Semele from Hades and raise her to Olympus; then, accompanied by a motley train of semi-human beings, maenads and panthers, he set off on wanderings throughout the world, from Libya to Arabia and India and back to his homeland. Everywhere he went he brought men knowledge of agriculture, arts and crafts, and especially of the vine and wine-making. On the isle of Naxos he discovered the Cretan princess Ariadne, abandoned there by Theseus, and made her his bride. Together they ascended to the heavens, whence he offers a similar blissful reward to his devotees, temporarily in this life and permanently after death.

If we follow – as I prefer – the Neoplatonists rather than the ethnographers in their interpretation of mythological personages, we find that they equate Dionysus with the 'mundane intellect', the Mind of this world. As son and heir of the cosmic creator Zeus, Dionysus is also a creative deity, but creative through thought, as it were. He produces the idea of the world, and his knowledge sustains it in all its reality. At the same time he is dismembered by the Titans, who are the direct creators of physical matter, and distributed into the human race, i.e. he is also the higher mind of each one of us. This higher intellect is a supernatural faculty of simultaneous creation, perception and understanding, through which man can gain supersensible knowledge. In the body it finds its reflection in the pineal gland (the 'third eye'), which cone-like organ atop the spinal column is represented by the thyrsus, that mysterious Bacchic wand made from a pine-cone fixed to a fennel stalk (see plates). The purpose of Bacchic initiation is presumably to awaken this faculty, and to make man aware of the great mind of which his intellect is a part. This is symbolized by the rebirth of Dionysus from an earthly mother, from which follow all the benefits which insight and creative inspiration have brought to mankind.

The connection of this metaphysical Dionysus with the notorious behaviour of his followers is not immediately apparent. Kerényi discusses only the phallic and sacrificial Dionysian rites of the earlier period, readily explained by his Indestructible Life theory. The Neoplatonists and their successors only consider the lofty, theological aspects. Evidently Dionysian religion embraced both extremes, just as Christianity includes Holy Rollers and Trappist monks. There were Bacchantes, no doubt, who, commemorating the act of the Titans, tore to pieces living creatures and devoured them raw. Doubtless there were some Dionysian initiations, specifically those of children, which revealed the 'facts of life' on a sexual level; while others, at the touch of the thyrsus, opened the window of the supersensible world. Perhaps the act of omophagy (eating raw flesh), under conditions of ritual intoxication, afforded a spiritual experience: we do not know, we who have not tried it. What is certain is that one insists at one's peril on fitting the Dionysian phenomena into a single, unifying theory of religious experience, substituting a tidy intellectual construct for a reality as vivid, as varied, and as unruly as the world itself.

97   *Dionysus and Pan*
Tapestry fragment from Egypt, fourth century A D. Boston, Museum of Fine Arts.

Although Dionysus himself is very rarely shown as ithyphallic, his association with Pan and the lustful retinue over which he presides show that he is a god of virility, fertility and the regenerative powers of sex. Pan carries here the pedum (shepherd's crook) and a fawn-skin, Dionysus a garland (cf. Pl. 100), while in the background are castanets, Pan-pipes and the kantharos drinking vessel, all Dionysian symbols. Both wear the haloes that denote divinity. Such crudely 'post-classical' works as the ones shown in this section bear witness to the survival of Dionysus' cult all around the Mediterranean well into the Christian era. But whether the persisting Dionysian iconography was supported by a continuation of his Mysteries is another question: they were probably limited to the great centres of urban civilization where his cult flourished most strongly, such as Alexandria, Athens, Pergamum and Ephesus.

Ivory pyxis, fifth century A D. Bologna,
Museo Civico Archeologico.

The young Dionysus squats confidently on
a throne, looking at himself in a mirror,
while two armed Corybantes, who should
be defending the infant god, prepare to kill
and dismember him. Dionysus' fascination
by a looking-glass, followed by his
temporary death, represents the fate of the
human soul which, according to Platonic
doctrine, looks down from its home in the
heavens and sees its reflection in the
deceptive surface of the material world.
Allured like Narcissus by the beauty of its
own image, it tries to grasp or follow the
evanescent vision, and in the effort tumbles
down into the miry toils of a life that is
death to the soul.

100 *Dionysus with the Seasons*
Sarcophagus, early third century AD. Kassel,
Landgrafenmuseum.

The god, riding a panther, is here flanked
by the four Seasons (cf. Pl. 9) and by putti
and fauns engaged in Dionysian activities.
He is a god of the cycles of the earth,
though historically this was expressed in an
unusual way. One year his death was
commemorated, the next year his
resurrection, in a two-year cycle of
Dionysian festivals. No reference to this is
to be seen in the Kassel sarcophagus, one of
the suavest products of its period which
invokes rather the late antique idea of the
Seasons as symbols of cosmic cycles, and of
the various saviour gods (including
Dionysus) as lords over them. The idea of
periodic death and rebirth is the
predominant meaning behind such an icon.

101 *Dionysus in India*
Sarcophagus, early third century AD. Kassel,
Landgrafenmuseum.

The two forms of the god are both shown
on this and several other sarcophagi in the
'Dionysian baroque' style. On the left is the
young god of the upper world, endowed
with the features of Alexander the Great –
another voyager to India and, so he claimed,
another son of Zeus by an earthly mother.
The serious elderly figure in the centre is the
god after his death going down to the
underworld: his placing suggests an
identification with the deceased. According
to Kerényi, the consecrated person or
animal representing Dionysus was
dismembered and eaten raw in a Mystery
commemorating the death of Dionysus
Zagreus and also affording (like the
Christian Mass) a communion for his
worshippers. The phallus alone was
preserved and it, or a wooden replica, was
placed in the liknon (see Pl. 106) to
represent the life-principle which would be
reborn the following year in the young
Dionysus, the 'light from the East'.

99 *The Lycurgus Cup*
Glass from Alexandria (?), *c.* AD 330–50.
London, British Museum.

With a craftsmanship verging on the
miraculous, the artist has carved on this cup
the tale of Dionysus' punishment of
Lycurgus, a Thracian king who molested
the followers of the god. On the reverse
Lycurgus is shown blinded and entangled in
the tendrils of a vine, while a faun and satyr
prepare to kill him at their master's
command. Why would such extraordinary
care have been lavished on this subject? It is
rare for Dionysus to be shown aggressive or
angry, and I can only conclude that the cup
was made, probably with magical as well as
decorative intent, in response to a
persecution of Dionysians and other pagans
by Christian fanatics, such as occurred
frequently in the Eastern Mediterranean
after Constantine's conversion.

102 Dionysus finds Ariadne
Mosaic from Merida, fifth or sixth century
A D. Merida, Museo Arqueológico.

Ariadne was abandoned by her lover
Theseus on the island of Naxos where
Dionysus found her, fell in love, and
married her. In southern Spain, at the very
close of antiquity, a local artist,
'Anniponus', was still using this subject:
Ariadne sleeping, a faun, a figure with
pedum and panther-skin, the god with toga,
hunting boots and kantharos. Did he know
the meaning, on any level, of what he was
depicting? Perhaps in his demesne Dionysus
had the status of a cargo-cult: a numinous
reminiscence of something
incomprehensible and obviously very
sacred, rather like the indigenous British
carvings of Roman and Oriental deities.

103 Triumph of Dionysus and Ariadne
Mosaic from Hadrumetum, early third
century A D. Tunisia, Sousse Museum.

The triumphal procession of a god with
attendant spirits always signifies a passage
through the states of existence, which is
naturally of most import in so far as it
concerns the fate of man. The soul is
Ariadne, the sleeping beauty abandoned by
her human lover Theseus (the physical
body) and swept off her feet by love of a
god. Borne on Dionysus' tiger-drawn
quadriga, she ascends with him to the sound
of maenadic music – the music of the
spheres – to her own proper realm, and his.
The Tunisian artist, unlike the one in
Merida (Pl. 102), was evidently copying
from a classical model.

104 The Old Dionysus visits a Mortal
Graeco-Roman copy of an Alexandrian
relief of the third century B C. London,
British Museum.

Ptolemy IV Philopator (*c.* 244–205 B C) was
a devotee of Dionysus and took the
organization of the cult in hand, actually
requiring all initiators to come to
Alexandria and register. In this relief,
probably dating from Ptolemy's time, the
old Dionysus, master of the underworld, is
figured, contrasting strongly in his *sobria
ebrietas* and his tipsy contingent with the

wide-awake welcoming gesture of his host.
We can tell from the box of masks beside
the couch that the latter is a poet or
dramatist, and of course he is not in bed but
at table. He is inviting Dionysus to a feast:
the sacred banquet of artistic production
and enjoyment. Well may he, awake to
the ordinary world, invoke the god of
subconscious inspiration whose altar stood
in every Greek theatre and who ruled both
the consummate art of tragedy and the lewd
satyr plays, the dramatizations of heroic
death and of tumescent life.

105 *Dionysian Cult Objects*

Wall-painting from Pompeii, first century AD. Naples, National Museum.

Most of the attributes of Dionysus are included here. At the top are a tambourine and a kantharos flanking a liknon, the wicker winnowing-basket in which the baby Dionysus was cradled, and which here contains another cup, a garlanded thyrsus, and a drinking horn draped with a panther-skin. On the steps are a sprig of bay, a pair of cymbals, and a miniature panther grappling with a snake. It would probably be a mistake to read too deep a meaning into this arrangement, but the contents of the liknon are interesting. Normally it is veiled; when unveiled it may contain fruits, a mask of Dionysus or a phallus, to the last of which the horn obviously alludes.

106 *The Liknon unveiled*
Terracotta relief, *c.* first century AD.
Hanover, Kestner Museum.

In this rare picture of an uncovered liknon, the basket is seen to contain the attributes of Priapus, an upright phallus placed among fruits, symbolizing the inexhaustible forces of life and fertility. Always in Dionysian initiation scenes, it is women who act as the leaders and initiators: the women (cf. Pl. 107) have control of the veiled men or boys who are evidently the neophytes. The liknon is brought by a silenus, i.e. by a non-human personage who stands outside the drama. In what, then consists the initiation? What is depicted here can only be a superficial part of the great Dionysian secret. The initiation must have been primarily a matter of the state of mind, and only secondarily one of content. The same ceremony, or symbols, witnessed in a state of religious or other intoxication, might have had a very different meaning and afforded a new intensity of experience, unsuspected by a mere beholder of the scene.

107 *Initiation Scene*
Stucco relief from the Farnesina, 30–25 BC.
Rome, National Museum.

As in Pl. 106, a woman leads a veiled male while a silenus attends to the liknon: here he is in the act of covering it. Kerényi says that in male initiations the liknon with its contents were put on the head of the man or boy, who thereby became a living symbol of the male principle. It may be that this individual was not actually initiated himself, but, like the boy in the Pompeian Villa of the Mysteries mural, merely acted a part for the benefit of a feminine ceremony. He is veiled so as not to see what the women actually do.

108 *Dionysian Revelry*
The silver 'Oceanus Dish' from the
Mildenhall Treasure, *c.* AD 350–75. London,
British Museum.

The outermost circle resounds with the
music of aulos and Pan-pipes, tambourines
and cymbals, as four lithe maenads dance
with Pan and his satyrs. Hercules is dead
drunk, his great bulk supported with
difficulty by two young attendants.
Dionysus alone is still, approached by his
consort, the more staidly moving Ariadne,
and served wine by a silenus. This is the
world of the blessed. The inner ring
contains again four 'couples', nymphs riding
sea-monsters. They are souls in transition,
crossing the 'ocean' which separates this
world from the next, and whose
personification as Oceanus (cf. Pl. 7)
occupies the centre.

109 *Dancing Maenads*
Roman funerary altar, mid-first century AD.
Rome, National Museum.

Two possible climaxes to a woman's
initiation were the sacred marriage with the
god, in which she identified with Ariadne,
and the ecstatic dance in which she became a
maenad. Music and movement, sexuality
and intoxication, all are implied in the
depictions of maenads, and from them the
Dionysia have earned the reputation they
have today. But when the dance appears on
a tombstone, it has nothing to do with
crude revelry: it has the same meaning as
the dance of the blessed souls with the
angels in the Christian paradise.

XIII *Orpheus and Hercules*

There might seem at first to be little in common between the gentle Thracian bard and the Argive strong-man. But unlike the subjects of the preceding chapters, Orpheus and Hercules were not gods, but mortal heroes who were elevated to Olympus after their deaths. Both were carried to Rome, moreover, on the same wave of Pythagorean enthusiasm that swept northwards from Magna Graecia at the end of the fourth century BC. At this period a statue of Pythagoras himself was erected at one end of the Comitium, and the cult of the Greek Heracles was permitted to enter the city. As the first foreign cult to do so, Hercules' had not a temple but an altar as its centre, the Ara Maxima. The Pythagoreans revered both heroes as having been inspired by Apollo, if indeed they were not actual incarnations of the Sun God. Hercules was also a focus of aspiration for the Stoics, who admired him alongside Ulysses as an exemplar of heroic virtue and constancy. The common people invoked him as an averter of evil and remover of obstacles, while several emperors encouraged his cult, with its stress on military virtues as an alternative to other licentious or over-mystical religions. Some of them identified themselves with him (see Commodus, p. 10), and the Emperor Julian hoped that Hercules might serve as a replacement for Christ.

Orpheus' was a more esoteric following. He seems to have lived in Thrace in post-Homeric but pre-classical times, and to have been a reformer of, and within, the cult of Dionysus. Like Christ in Judaism and Buddha in Hinduism, he was rejected by followers of the old faith but succeeded in founding a new one alongside it. Orphism is an ascetic and speculative Dionysianism, aiming at the same goal of release from earthly conditions but pursuing it in a more conscious, controlled and intellectual way. Pythagoras' own school is the perfect example of Orphic attitudes, and coeval with the first evidence of Orphic activities in Athens and southern Italy. With the Neopythagorean revival of the last centuries BC came the establishment of a literary canon (the Orphic Hymns), an elaborate theogony and cosmogony, and Mysteries among whose initiates were Plutarch and, some say, the young Saul of Tarsus. The ascetic teachings of the

Orphics, so very foreign to the Greek mentality, were perfectly at one with early Christian ethics, and the figure of Orpheus was borrowed in Christian iconography for representations of David and even of Christ himself. Certainly the two religions seem to have coalesced in certain circles (see Pl. 110).

Orpheus, Hercules and Jesus: all three were born as demi-gods, performed miracles, and descended to the underworld before or after suffering cruel deaths. They were afterwards raised to Heaven by their divine fathers, whence they still radiate beneficent influences to their worshippers. Which of them one would have chosen in the early centuries AD would depend on one's own inner orientation. The Orphic life of ascesis and intellectual learning would appeal to those on the Path of Knowledge, and they would understand best the doctrines of reincarnation and eventual liberation from the Circle of Necessity through one's own efforts. Christ, on the other hand, is the perfect exemplar of the Path of Divine Love, and Hercules of the Path of the Warrior, the way of selfless activity and ceaseless labours in the cause of the good.

110 *Orphic Signet-ring*
Gold ring, fifth century AD. London, British Museum.

The Greek inscription around the edge of the bezel reads ΤΟ ΣΦΡΑΓΗΣ Ο ΟΑΝΟU ΤΟU ΑΓΗΟU ΦΘΑΝΗ – probably to be translated as 'The Seal of John, the Pre-eminent Saint'. In the centre Orpheus is seated, playing the lyre, while a serpent curls round a tree and two indeterminate beasts lie at his feet. The actual meaning and provenance of the ring are a mystery, but it seems to assimilate Orpheus with St John the Divine. Whatever his ancient nature, 'Orpheus' was acknowledged by late pagans as the theologian *par excellence*; and certainly the theology of St John, of all the Christian canon, is most readily reconciled with the highest pagan doctrines. The seal probably comes from syncretistic Christian circles in which Orpheus was recognized as the pre-eminent 'saint' of the pagan world.

111 *Orpheus with Seven-stringed Lyre*
Mosaic from Vienne. Vienne, Lapidarium
St-Pierre.

Orpheus plays the same instrument as his
father Apollo, symbolizing the music of the
seven planets and the universal laws of
septenary manifestation whose knowledge
gives magical power over all created things.
Orpheus could charm beasts, plants and
even the denizens of the Underworld, i.e. he
understood the laws of sympathy and
harmony that link every level of creation,
and was able to put them to use. Whether
this is done through actual music or through
alchemy, astrology or magic makes little
difference, these being man-made categories
that, like the various religions, divide an
essential unity in order to accommodate the
differences within the human race.

112 *Orpheus charming the Beasts*
Ivory pyxis, fourth century AD. Bobbio,
San Colombano.

The creatures are the same as take part in
the processions of Dionysus: faun, centaur,
lion, goat, etc. (see Pl. 101). But in contrast
to the noise and revelry of the Bacchic rout,
around Orpheus all is stillness and silence
save his music. Just so, the historical
Orpheus tamed the rites of Dionysus,
rejecting the cruel and undisciplined
elements and imposing – perhaps for the
first time in the Western world – a lofty
ethic of purity and non-injury. The Orphics
and Pythagoreans were truly the first
Christians in the ethical sense, and a few
Christians like St Francis have extended
their compassion in Pythagorean fashion to
the animal kingdom.

113 *Herculean Initiate*
Marble funerary statue from Massicault,
later third century AD. Tunis, Bardo
National Museum.

Clad in the Nemean lionskin and grasping a
bunch of poppies, the initiate takes on the
guise of Hercules at the end of his career,
after his initiation into the Eleusinian
Mysteries. The finely-drawn portrait of a
serious older man contrasts strangely with
the ill-proportioned body, but there is
something touching about his markedly un-
Herculean physique. From his face he seems
a far more plausible candidate for mystical
initiations than a crude muscle-man such as
the famous Farnese Hercules. The poppies
suggest that the Eleusinian Mysteries, like
those of Dionysus, may have involved the
use of drugs. But we cannot assume that
they had the same effect on the ancients as
they do today, for the psyche of man and
his relationship to the unseen worlds have
definitely altered since those times.

114 *The Labours of Hercules*
Sarcophagus, c. AD 150. Velletri, Museo
Civico.

Hercules' first four labours all entailed
slaying troublesome beasts: the Nemean
Lion, whose pelt he wore for ever after; the
Lernaean Hydra; the Erymanthian Boar;
and the Stymphalian Birds. The next four
involved live animals: the capture of the
Ceryneian Hind; the cleaning of the
Augean Stables (for which Hercules should
have received a tithe of Augeas' herd); the
capture of the Cretan Bull and of the Mares
of Diomedes. His last four adventures were
to capture the Girdle of Hippolyte, the
Cattle of Geryon, the Golden Apples of the
Hesperides, and Cerberus, the guard-dog of
the Underworld. In occult circles these
labours are said to symbolize the twelve
trials through which the soul of Everyman
must pass before it is released from the
bonds of earthly existence and the need for
further incarnations. On a sarcophagus they
imply the identification of the deceased with
the hero, and express a hope that his life and
labours will also end with assimilation to the
gods.

115 *Apotheosis of Hercules*
Tower-tomb of the Secundini, *c.* AD 245. Igel, near Trier.

Hercules' last adventure trapped him into donning the blood-soaked shirt of the centaur Nessus, whom he had killed. As soon as he wore it a terrible burning seized him, but he could not get it off. Tearing up pine-trees in his agony, he built with them a funeral pyre, and as the flames reached his body he was snatched up to heaven by his father Zeus. Here he ascends in a chariot, to be received by his patroness Athena, in the apotheosis which awaits all heroes at the end of their trials on earth.

XIV *The Overseers*

The wise pagan Celsus thought it probable that from the beginning the different parts of the earth had been allotted to different overseers, and that it was thus entirely proper for men to worship their own local gods and goddesses. Being a Platonic philosopher, Celsus did not confuse these lesser gods, daemons, angels, folk-souls (call them what you will) with the Supreme God. But local pride and provincialism tended to blur the distinction in the minds of many. It is inevitable among unphilosophical people, and in general there is no harm done by identifying one's overseer with the Absolute, any more than in treating one's family as if they were the most important people in the world. In this section we pass in review some ten of these beings. Most of them are quite a mystery to modern researchers, since there are no records of their doctrines and rituals. Fragmentary inscriptions and occasional mentions in literature are all we have to supplement the iconography and architectural remains in which they appear in all their glory.

Roman Syria stretched from the Taurus Mountains to the Euphrates, and every region had its own local pantheon whose head was the Lord of Heaven. These are the 'gods of the heathen' of the Old Testament, and their nature is well illustrated in I Kings 18 where Elijah and the prophets of Baal compete for a celestial thunderbolt to kindle their offerings: they are at once supercosmic powers and telluric weather gods. Hence their eagles and thunderbolts, symbols of unsurpassable heights and irresistible magical power. When the Romans annexed Syria in 64 BC they encouraged the inhabitants to equate their various overseers with Jupiter: the Jupiter Optimus Maximus or even the Jupiter Exsuperantissimus around whom all the other Roman deities were tending to revolve. For the Romans such assimilation was an easy matter, but in fact there was much variety in the Syrian religion, and many vestiges of a more primordial cult which they overlooked in their synthesizing enthusiasm. Some of the gods reacted by imposing their religions on their conquerors, in cults that stretched from one end of the Empire to the other.

One such was the god of Dolichenus (Pls 116–119), who had his territory in Commagene, a small area now in southern Turkey which the Romans added to Syria in AD 72. From these obscure beginnings his influence spread along the Danube and the Rhine, through the Netherlands and up to Hadrian's Wall. Syria was the most fertile source of slaves and soldiers in an expanding economy that felt an increasing need for both, and these were probably the first to propagate his cult. But as provincials were promoted and given citizenship, so also Dolichenus climbed the social ladder, gaining adherents among senators and knights and reaching his apogee in the time of the Severi around AD 200. In contrast to the dedications by individuals to Mithras, the other favourite god of the legionaries, Dolichenus received votive dedications from entire units, suggesting that his was a more open and exoteric cult, probably without any profound initiatic content although its symbols are deeply rooted in Aryan tradition.

The overseers of the Syrian tribes all bore the name Bel or Baal, and like Dolichenus fulfilled both the position of a supreme deity above the cosmos – Baal Shamin, 'Lord of Heaven' – and that of an approachable and personal father and weather god. Many inscriptions in Palmyra address Baal, like his successor Allah, as 'the Compassionate and Merciful', and record gratitude 'because the God listened to the prayer'. But there was also in Syria and throughout the ancient Near East a cult of non-anthropomorphic symbols of the overseers: a cult of stones and mountain-tops, of totems and star-lore. High places are always associated with the Sky God: they encourage observation of the stars and planets, and afford contact with elemental forces; in them one feels elevated above the human condition, unprotected but also unencumbered by the everyday life of the valleys beneath. They are peculiarly the haunts of local overseers and have always been recognised as holy. Sacred stones also come from the sky. Meteorites, regarded as actual thunderbolts, are gifts from the Lord of Heaven, and just as the local Baals are in a sense lesser reflections of him, so the meteorite is a fragment of heaven and is revered as such. Examples which have affected more than local history are the Ka'ba Stone at Mecca; the meteoric image of Cybele at Pessinus; and the Betyl of Emesa (modern Homs) which the Emperor Elagabalus brought in triumph to Rome in his attempt to force the entire Empire into obeisance before the local Baal of which he happened to be high priest (see Pl. 35).

All the Baals have female consorts, at least in theory: they are not often shown as a reigning pair. These are the *saktis* of the gods in

Hindu theology, meaning the power with which a god, otherwise self-contained, 'procreates' and thus creates and influences lower levels of being. Baal Hadad of Hierapolis (now Membij) in north Syria had a notable consort in Atargatis, known to the Greeks and Romans simply as the 'Syrian Goddess'. Lucian has left a vivid account of her festivals, which included the raising of gigantic phalli, people swimming out to deck an altar in the middle of a sacred lake, the sacrifice of animals, and self-mutilation. It was just such religious enthusiasms that St Paul found so repulsive at Ephesus, where the Ephesian Artemis had one of the most magnificent Ionic temples of the ancient world. Here and in other centres of Asia Minor – Aphrodisias, Samos, Sardis, Pergamum – the inhabitants seem to have favoured goddesses, who presided over their development in Hellenistic and Roman times until their cities became bywords for elegance and luxury.

Sometimes the Great Goddess has as her consort not a mature Zeus-type but a younger man, perhaps her son. Cybele and Attis are the best-known example; in Anatolia and Phrygia there was also Men, a moon god, who had important centres near modern Antalya at which it appears that the Mysteries involved a sacred marriage ceremony. There is a tradition, probably the oldest one of all, that the moon is not female but male and that it is the Man in the Moon, not the husband, who really impregnates women – for in primitive societies sexual intercourse is not necessarily connected causally with pregnancy. A modern resurgence of this belief is the method of birth-control by considering the relation of the phase of the moon to the woman's natal horoscope: conception is most likely when the sun and moon are in the same relationship as at her birth. So old superstitions are modernized and reborn, and so the celebration of the hierogamy of Men and the Great Mother Goddess may have had a practical as well as a ritual purpose.

Sabazius, originating in Thrace (now Bulgaria), is another local overseer of whom very little is known nowadays. As with Men and so many others, his remains are from later epochs – Hellenistic and later – by which time he had undergone assimilation and no doubt distortion. The Greeks equated him with Dionysus, the Romans at first with Bacchus then, in the increasingly syncretistic atmosphere of the Empire period, with the same cosmocratic Jupiter as had swallowed up the individual Baals. Sabazius' symbols are the snake and the pine-cone, and this is enough to indicate that he was an initiatic god and not merely a tribal totem. They symbolize the Kundalini and the Third Eye, with which the true Mysteries concern themselves. According to Clement of Alexandria, the Sabazian Mysteries involved drawing a live serpent across the breast of the initiate in imitation, he says, of the 'God who penetrates the bosom'. Here is a clear example of a ritual action, seemingly bizarre, paralleling an interior experience in the heart-centre: 'an outward and visible sign of an inward and spiritual grace'.

116   *Standard of Dolichenus*
Bronze standard from Mauer, second century AD. Vienna, Kunsthistorisches Museum.

Several triangular standards, no two alike, show Jupiter Dolichenus with his consort Juno Dolichena. Many of them seem rather confused in imagery, but this one is quite plain in its arrangement of the pair on four different levels of being. At the apex is the Dolichene triad of eagle, sun and moon, i.e. the hypercosmic principle which is Jupiter in his highest manifestation, above the symbols of the opposites in the cosmos. Next are Jupiter and Juno in their respective bull- and stag-drawn chariots, symbols of the dynamic action of solar and lunar, or of positive and negative, influences. Below these the pair perform a sacrifice: the perpetual transmutation of matter and energy that sustains the world. At the bottom they both stand on bulls, flanked by army standards and facing a statue of Victory, representing their personal function as givers of good fortune and success.

117　*Jupiter Dolichenus on his Bull*
Bronze statuette. Vienna, Kunsthistorisches
Museum.

The Dolichene supreme god wears a
military cuirass not so much because he is a
war god as because this was the usual
ceremonial garb of emperors on earth. His
weapon, the double-headed axe, is one of
the most venerable symbolic arms, found
wherever the Aryan race has spread, from
Tibet to Scandinavia. It refers to the duality
of constructive and destructive forces (both
of which an axe can serve) that govern the
manifested world. Then it is equivalent to
the thunderbolt (resembling in shape the
Indian *vajra* or Tibetan *dorje*) which is
peculiarly the attribute of cosmic or sky
gods. Ancient people recognized the
lightning-stroke as a life-bringing force, and
modern scientists have expressed the same
idea in their fantasies about the origins of
organic compounds from the action of
lightning on some primeval molecular
'broth'. Finally the ceremonial axe is
traditionally of stone (e.g. the Cretan *labrys*)
and hence an incarnation – or rather a
petrification – of a spiritual principle.
Dolichenus' beasts are the eagle and the bull,
the former associated with Jupiter as
hypercosmic principle, the latter with the
sign of Taurus. This places his origins far
anterior to any of his monuments, among
the other cosmocrators of the Taurean Age
(fourth-third millennia BC), such as Varuna
and the Cretan Zeus.

< 118 *Plaque of Dolichenus*
Silver plaque with traces of gilding, from
Heddernheim, second-third century AD.
London, British Museum.

The inscription dedicates this finely-beaten
plaque to 'I[upiter] O[ptimus] M[aximus]
Dolicheno ubi ferrum nascitur' – 'where
the iron is born' – referring to the iron
mines of Doliche. Its shape suggests the Sky
God's thunderbolt. Several other tablets
showing a god in identical stance and
surroundings have been found in England,
but dedicated to Mars, who is even more
closely associated with iron, since his planet
rules the metal and the weapons made of it.
The virtue of the god is inherent in the
metal, and in response to the soldier's
offering will aid its user.

119   *Dolichenus and Egyptian Divinities*
Relief from the Dolichene shrine on the
Aventine, second century AD. Rome,
Capitoline Museum.

The main elements here are the traditional
Dolichene symbols: Jupiter and Juno on
bull and hind, the wreathed and flaming
altar, the eagle with a thunderbolt. At the
corners are the two Dioscuri, Castor and
Pollux, whose origins lie in ancient Roman
religion but who often attend Dolichenus.
More surprising are the busts, in the centre,
of Serapis and Isis. Theirs is the place of
honour, perhaps in acknowledgment of
them as superior manifestations of the male
and female powers, like Sol and Luna in
Pl. 116.

120   *A Palmyrene Trinity*
Niche lintel from the sanctuary of Baal
Shamin, first century A D. Syria, Palmyra
Museum.

Baal Shamin, Lord of Heaven, is
represented by an eagle, overshadowing his
two cohorts Aglibol and Malakbel, the
moon and sun gods. They each have their
own eagles, indicating cosmic powers
similar in kind to Baal Shamin's, but
inferior in degree. Little is known of
Palmyrene religion, except the propitiatory
parts of it: sacrifices and thank-offerings.
But it included sacred banquets of a
eucharistic kind at which wine was drunk,
always a symbol of hidden Mysteries; and
inside the richly decorated tombs not only
are the deceased shown feasting, but
communion meals were celebrated by the
living.

121   *Malakbel in Griffin Chariot*
Altar from Palmyra. Rome, Capitoline
Museum.

Malakbel is the Palmyrene Sun God, carried
heavenwards here by the archetypal solar
animals, half-lion, half-eagle. The sun that
we see in the sky is merely the wheel of the
solar chariot, revolving as it climbs up to
the zenith at noon, then plunging at sunset
into the desert or the sea. The solar orb is
propelled by invisible forces, represented by
these four mythical creatures, who provide
its motive power much as the four great
Archangels oversee this earth and keep it on
its course. But directing these powers is a
single being, the Soul of the Sun or Solar
Logos, and it is he who is represented by the
person in the chariot.

122 Zeus-Baal Shamin
Relief from Dura Europos, AD 32. Yale University Art Gallery.

This stele is dated and inscribed in Greek 'to Zeus' and in Palmyrene Aramaic 'to Baal Shamin'. It shows Zeus crowned like Serapis with a modius and figuring as a giver of fruits to mankind. The donor offers him a sheep. Dura Europos, now Qalat es Sālihiya on the Syrian Euphrates, is an important source for monuments of several religions (see also Pls 47, 68, 71), but its local lord was Baal Shamin, the universal deity of the Syrian tribes.

123 The 'Boglio Stele'
Limestone relief from Siliana, late third century AD. Tunis, Bardo National Museum.

Baal Hammon of Carthage was assimilated to the Roman Saturn, named on this funerary stele, and appropriately so for he is the 'grim reaper': the lord of the harvest and the harvester of men. The dedicator Cuttinus and his wife were Punic landowners, and the lower compartments show their activities in life: ploughing, harvesting, and offering their best produce to the gods. Saturn is a beneficent figure, sickle in hand, mounted on a bull like other Baals. The Dioscuri stand on either side, lords of the dawn and twilight and hence guardians of the passage between heaven and earth. Two Victories and an eagle complete the picture: the eagle, perhaps, of Jupiter Exsuperantissimus who reigns even above the realm of his father Kronos, in the timeless state where reaping and winnowing are no more.

124 *Atargatis*
Statue from the Janiculum, third century
A D. Rome, National Museum.

This statue, evidently influenced both by
Egyptian art and by the spiralling serpent
motif of the Mithraic Aion (see Pls 72, 74),
is probably intended to represent the Syrian
Goddess, Atargatis of Hierapolis. Her cult
had the same appeal for the Romans as the
other exotic religions from the East: a ritual
aimed at self-forgetfulness and self-
abnegation in the face of a consuming
divinity. Sacred prostitution was practised at
her Syrian centre, though not at Rome,
affording communion with the goddess
through intercourse with her earthly
representative.

125 *Artemis of Ephesus*
Statue from the Prytaneion, Ephesus, later
second century A D. Izmir, Selçuk Museum.

The original 'Diana of the Ephesians' was a
wooden statue clothed in gold, which
according to Pliny survived through seven
successive rebuildings of her fabulous
temple. All the detailed representations of
her, however, date from a late period – after
A D 200 – and show various accretions,
canonical or invented. No two are exactly
the same. Her invariable attributes are the
tight garment that encases her to the ankles,
almost like a herm, its panels filled with
animal and other symbols, and the very
complicated hauberk which blossoms out
below breast level into many egg-like
protuberances. In this example its
decorations include a Zodiac necklace, and
on the back of her head there is a crescent
moon. Her hands were open, in a
welcoming gesture. Whether the curious
appendages are in fact meant as breasts,
justifying her epithet 'Diana multimamma',
or whether they have some other meaning,
even the best scholars cannot decide. Are
they grapes, eggs or the offerings of her
Galli? The overall effect is one of (literally)
exuberant life.

126 *Aphrodite of Aphrodisias*
Statue from Aphrodisias (?). Vienna,
Kunsthistorisches Museum.

Obviously a close cousin of the Ephesian
Artemis, the goddess of Aphrodisias shows
signs of a more contrived decorative
schema. Here is nothing grotesque or
enigmatic, but standard motifs of the
Hellenistic and Roman periods: a crescent,
the three Graces, the Sun and Moon, and
Aphrodite riding a sea-goat (Capricorn).
Sometimes the order varies, and a panel of
Erotes is added at the bottom. The meaning
is clear: she is a cosmic goddess, like the
Baals and Jupiter; she rules the Sun and
Moon, and disperses her gifts via the trinity
of Graces; she rules the sea and hence the
world of the unconscious, and causes men to
love.

127 *Artemis-Anahita and Apollo*
Stele from Izmir. Leiden, Rijksmuseum.

Anahita was an ancient Persian goddess 'of
the fertilizing waters', whose humid
influences, pouring down from the heavens,
gave fecundity to the earth. In Armenia the
daughters of noble families would go to her
temples to prostitute themselves before their
marriage: a ceremony of dedication which
also ensured some genetic mixture.
Anahita's cult spread westwards throughout
Asia Minor, where she was interpreted now
as Cybele, now as Artemis or as Aphrodite.
Here her figure is unmistakably that of
Ephesian Artemis, and she is paired with her
brother Apollo as sun and moon deities.
Both are placed in niches, like the sacred
betyl-stones of Syria. The combination of
niche with pediment is frequently found as a
model of the 'House of God', a miniature
temple in itself (see Pl. 131).

128 Men
Bronze statuette. Leiden, Rijksmuseum.

Men was the Moon God of Anatolia and
Phrygia. He was assimilated to Attis, with
whom he shares his Phrygian cap and
youthful good looks, but he was originally a
greater god: self-created, higher than the
sun, ruler of heaven, earth and the
underworld. His symbols are the peacock,
pomegranate and pine-cone, all referring to
death and rebirth: functions with which the
moon is closely connected as the first station
for the ascending, and the last for the
descending, soul.

129 Sabazian Hand
Bronze hand, third-fourth century A D. St
Louis, Missouri, City Art Museum.

Many bronze hands of this kind have been
found, all in the logos-gesture (see Pl. 56)
but varying greatly in the number and
nature of the symbols attached to them. A
few are altogether bare. Some have a snake
or a pine-cone, Sabazius' particular
attributes. Others have the figures of other
'Jupiters' – Heliopolitanus and Dolichenus.
Several such as this one are crammed with
figures, animals and symbolic objects. Their
sheer variety deters one from any but the
vaguest generalizations as to their meanings,
but it seems that they were self-contained
objects of a votive nature, expressing like
the Sabazian plaque (Pl. 130) the centrality
of the god's logos or thought to all creation.
In this specimen there is a noticeable and
perhaps significant division into three levels:
on the wrist, a cavern containing a mother
and child (cf. Pl. 138) and supporting an
altar; in the centre, the figure of Sabazius
himself; on the outstretched fingers,
perched on a thunderbolt, the eagle of the
cosmocrator with the broken bust (of
Ganymede?) on its wing. Perhaps Sabazius
is invoked here as a saviour god, mediating
between the dark cavern of generation and
the empyrean heights.

130 Sabazius
Bronze relief found in Rome, first century
A D. Copenhagen, National Museum.

The assortment of objects and creatures
surrounding the Phrygian-capped Sabazius
includes recognized divinities: the Dioscuri,
Helios in a quadriga, the Sun and Moon;
symbolic animals: fly, mouse, bull, tortoise,
bee, locust, frog, eagle on pillar, serpent,
lizard; objects: scales, ox haunch, two
crossed auloi, winged lightning, yoke,
several vessels, rosettes, cornucopia,
cymbals, ear of barley, plough. The
crowding together of so many symbols
resembles syncretistic images (see
Chapter XV), but few of them have definite
connections with particular gods. They are
not doctrinal allusions so much as
apotropaic and sympathetic invocations,
made in a magical frame of mind.

131 Dedication to the Moon God
Stele, possibly from Thessaloniki. Istanbul, Archaeological Museum.

The maker of this stele, like those of the objects in Pls 123, 127 and 130, is following a traditional pattern of universal significance. Fundamentally a combination of a triangle and a square, it is a symbol of the heavens, where the superhuman beings proliferate in triads or trinities, above the earth, where all is compounded of the four elements. In the Boglio and Anahita stelae there is the added refinement of a dome in between the two, representing the vault of the visible heavens and containing the lord of that limited universe. The triangular pediment is above the inerratic circle of the stars, and contains the eagle of hypercosmic Jupiter. This stele fills the middle zone, unusually, with the Moon God, the three Fates, Men and Hercules. The donors, as in the Boglio stele, are firmly on 'earth'. This threefold scheme of the celestial, planetary and elemental worlds is found throughout the Perennial Philosophy, and is a key to many varieties of traditional architecture, beside being reflected in the human body itself.

132 Winged City Goddess
Silver statuette from Macon, France, before AD 260. London, British Museum.

Cities as well as nations have their fates, personified as tutelary deities to whom the generic name of Tyche (Fate) was given. This figure may be the Tyche of Marsilia – now Marseilles. Just as every human being is a microcosm, so every lesser god or goddess is supreme in his or her own preserve, and contains elements of the archetypal inferior gods. The ruler of a city has seven aspects which correspond to the planets, shown here above her head in order of the days of the week: Saturn, Sun, Moon, Mars, Mercury, Jupiter, Venus. Beneath these are the Dioscuri, and at her left hand the twins Apollo and Artemis. With her right hand she pours a libation upon an altar, presumably sacrificing to those greater powers of which she is an image.

XV *Syncretism*

Every now and then the currents of history force people out of their insularity and compel them to recognize that there are others in the world whose habits and customs differ utterly from their own. This took place on a large scale under the Roman Empire, when innumerable individuals were uprooted through slavery or for military purposes; and again in our own time Westerners, at least, have been driven by inquisitiveness and ambition to explore the whole earth. A broadening of human horizons is the happiest result of such compulsions – of the unhappy results enough has been said by others – and such expansion of consciousness affects most powerfully the ever-sensitive nerve of religion.

Two basic reactions are possible: that of the missionary and that of the syncretist. The missionary, fired by the conviction that his is the only true god, or that his faith is the best one for all men, seeks to impose it upon less favoured folk by example, argument, subterfuge or force. Sometimes he goes so far as to believe himself endowed by evolution – or even entrusted by God – with the right to rule these 'lesser breeds without the law'. But the Romans, for all their faults, did not share the contempt for other races that was so marked among the Athenians and the Jews, for example. They were conquerors, of course, arrogant and greedy for territory; but once a land was subject to them their custom was, increasingly, to grant the free inhabitants Roman citizenship with all its privileges and opportunities. Their attitude to religion was similarly tolerant, though it was admittedly the tolerance of agnosticism and convenience: for religion was a powerful means for the assimilation of other cultures. If you respect a man's gods, you are half-way towards winning his friendship.

Politics rather than philosophy lay behind the early syncretistic attitude, which simply juxtaposed the gods of different cultures or else equated them. The Romans had been doing this from their earliest days as the masters of Italy, admitting first the local overseers of other Italic tribes and then Latinizing in its entirety Greek Olympus. Later the Syrian Baals all became Jupiters, as described in the previous chapter, and provincial pantheons like those of the Celts and Gauls were enriched by the enrolment of suitable Greek or Roman gods.

A second stage of syncretism grew out of an increasing impulse towards monotheism, felt throughout the Empire towards the beginning of the Christian era. Perhaps it surfaced first in the cult of Isis, who was already a universal goddess in her homeland of Egypt. The Egyptians had cultivated solar and other monotheisms for thousands of years, and their conceptions and knowledge of deity far surpassed those of younger nations. The Isiac syncretists would accept a multiplicity of powers in the universe, yet subject them to a One who is their centre, or apex. The personification of the One, in later syncretisms, could be the Sun, or it could be a named god or goddess (see Pls 136 and 138–141), upon whom were bestowed as attributes the symbols of other gods, as many as possible. This implies that the chosen divinity includes all the others as its powers and aspects. It is an acknowledgment of the reality of other gods, but expresses a preference – perhaps merely a personal, not a dogmatic one – for one's own.

Syncretism, while preferable to bigotry and persecution, was never more than a convenience, at a low philosophical level. Rather like the modern democratic attitude which allows everyone's opinion equal weight, it makes no attempt at a real 'discerning of spirits', i.e. at trying to establish the actual nature and function of each god, which, if it can be done, ineluctably places them in a hierarchy. The Neoplatonists used the names of Greek and Roman gods to expound the complexities of their hierarchical scheme of 'Orphic' theology, but the scheme must have existed long before, expressed in symbols of another sort. The beings to which they refer as 'Jupiter', 'Attis', etc., are not necessarily the same as the ones which were commonly worshipped under those names: yet these philosophers alone give us insight into an esoteric theology, without which we would be little better off than the simple syncretists.

133 *Cernunnos with Apollo and Mercury*
Relief from Rheims, early first century AD.
Rheims, Museum.

The Celtic Cernunnos is a god of the underworld and the dead, and also of healing and wealth, combining worldly and subterranean functions like the Greek Pluto. Acceptance of him contributed greatly to the success of the Romanization of Gaul. The Celtic belief, at least in exoteric circles, was that the dead live in a world beneath the earth: a world of compensation and wish-fulfilment, rather more inviting than the twilit limbo of Hades. Wealth and happiness on earth were a foretaste of these undying pleasures. Cernunnos pours forth a stream of gold coins as he sits cross-legged between his familiar animals: the destructive rat above, the beneficent bull and stag below. These are the same beasts as the steeds of Juno and Jupiter Dolichenus (Pl. 116) and their presence here may serve to 'place' Cernunnos in the same traditional mainstream of Taurean overseers. Quite incongruous with the rough, trousered and horned god are his two supporters, a very classically poised Apollo and Mercury. But if the prime attribute of Cernunnos is seen to be his riches, then their functions are complementary to his: Mercury is traditionally bringer of wealth, and Apollo is the Sun God, hence the ruler of all things golden.

134 *Osiris-Ammon-Serapis*
Bronze statuette from Karanis, Egypt, late third-early fourth century A D. University of Michigan, Kelsey Museum of Archaeology.

The three greatest gods of Egypt were Osiris of Abydos, Ammon of Thebes, and Serapis of Alexandria. Osiris' white crown of Upper Egypt surmounts the ram's horns of Ammon on the head of this figure, whose noble head and ample garments mark him as Serapis. His arms are in the position of the famous seated Serapis of Bryaxis (see Pl. 88), and would presumably have held staff and thunderbolt, the latter connecting him with Zeus and all other sky gods.

135 *Mercury, Cybele, Attis and Sabazius*
Bronze diptych, second century A D. Berline, Staatliche Museen.

The origins of this plaque are unknown, but it would seem to be similar in intention to some diptychs of medieval Christian art which depict various favourite saints. An individual in a syncretistic environment might well form an affection for four assorted deities: Sabazius as father, Cybele as mother, Mercury as helper, and Attis as saviour. And when one considers the varied genesis of Catholic saints, then the parallel is quite close: some are historical individuals, certainly, but others are legendary figures or even transmuted pagan divinities; and they come from all over the known world.

136 *Dedication to the Moon God, Men*
Stele from Dorylaeum, second-third
century AD (?) Formerly in the British
Museum, London.

137 *Cake-mould with Pantheistic Symbols*
From Taranto, fourth century AD. Oxford,
Ashmolean Museum. (Cast only shown.)

138 *Sabazian Mother Goddess and Child*
Bronze statuette, second century AD.
Boston, Museum of Fine Arts.

139 *Dionysus and Ariadne ascending in a
Quadriga*
Terracotta disc from Brindisi, fourth-first
century BC. Brindisi, Museo Provinciale.

140 *Venus adjusting her Sandal at a Trellis*
Bronze statuette, second century AD.
London, British Museum.

141 *Goddess with Elephant Head-dress*
Silver plaque from Boscoreale, third
century BC–first century AD. Paris, Louvre.

Six 'pantheistic' images, very disparate in
time and place, illustrate a tendency to
crowd every possible symbol into a single
image. All except Pl. 137 are centred around
a particular anthropomorphic deity. The
symbols found on these objects, some many
times but others only once, are as follows:

Atlantes
Bow: Apollo
Bull: Moon God or Cosmocrator
Caduceus: Mercury
Cap: Phrygian deities
Chous vessel: Dionysus
Corn ear: Demeter
Cornucopia: Tellus or Pluto
Crescent: Luna
Crosstorch: Demeter and Persephone
Cymbals: Cybele
Dioscuri (Castor and Pollux)
Distaff: Fates
Dolphin: Apollo
Eagle: Jupiter or Sky God
Elephant: Dionysus
Eros
Frog
Goat: Pan
Goblets
Hammer: Vulcan
Helios
Ladder: Adonis
Liknon: Dionysus

Lion: Cybele
Lyre: Apollo
Mercury
Mirror: Venus
Moon: Luna
Panther: Dionysus
Peacock: Juno
Pedum: Attis
Pine-cone: Attis, Dionysus,
    Sabazius, Men
Pipes (syrinx): Pan
Purse: Mercury
Quiver: Apollo
Ram
Raven
Rudder: Fortuna
Salamander
Sickle: Saturn
Sistrum: Isis
Snake: Aesculapius, Sabazius
Stars
Stork
Sun
Tambourine: Cybele
Thunderbolt: Jupiter
Thyrsus: Dionysus
Tongs: Vulcan
Torch: Hecate or Dioscuri
Tortoise: Mercury
Trident: Neptune
Wheel: Tyche
Zodiac

142 *Phanes Cosmocrator*
Relief, late second century A D. Modena,
Museum.

This magnificent figure has given rise to
much debate. Cumont identified him as
Aion (see Pls 72–74) from his wings and
serpent; Eisler as the Orphic first-born god
Phanes Protogonus, who sprang from the
primeval egg; Nilsson as a nameless
syncretistic god of all the heavenly bodies, a
typical representative of second-century
syncretism. Certainly he seems to be
emerging in flames from the sundered
halves of Phanes' egg, above his head and
below his feet. The other visible symbols are
solar rays and a lunar crescent behind his
head and shoulders; masks of ram, lion and
goat on his torso; thunderbolt and staff in
his hands (the attributes of Serapis) and
cloven hooves for feet, like Pan. Around
him are the familiar circle of the Zodiac and
the square of the Winds (cf. Pl. 67). The
inscription 'Felix Pater', and an erased
female name, suggests a Mithraic
environment, thereby seeming to support
the identification as Aion.

According to the Orphic system, all the
higher gods have their manifestations on
lower levels: so that, according to
Damascius, even Phanes, also called Pan, has
a mundane existence as the chief of all local
overseers – the principle from which they
all depend. But this figure is not actually
shown at the mundane, but at the cosmic
level: he fills the whole Zodiac, wielding
the powers of all its gods. The Orphics
identify this manifestation of Phanes with
the demiurgic Jupiter, the 'mingler of all
things', namely of the pure archetypal
qualities into the world's elements, gross
and subtle. Phanes-Jupiter is encircled by the
serpent of Time, to which his ideas become
subject when they enter the manifested and
visible world, depicted here by a Zodiac
circle compressed to a mandorla (like that
which surrounds the Cosmic Christ in
Majesty in medieval paintings). In its
multiple ramifications and the profundity of
its symbolism – to which I am not prepared
to do justice – the Modena Phanes may be
regarded as the ultimate in Mystery
iconography.

Select Bibliography

A complete bibliography of the Mystery religions would be immense. In selecting the following list of titles, I have in mind the non-academic reader who wishes to pursue the subject further, rather than the scholar who has the sources already at his disposal. Hence the disproportionate number of titles in English. For the specialist with a command of three or four languages it is sufficient to mention the series of studies published by E. J. Brill of Leiden, under the general editorship of Professor M. J. Vermaseren, modestly entitled *Études Préliminaires aux Religions Orientales dans l'Empire Romain*. Already numbering over eighty titles, many of them sets of two or more volumes, this tremendous undertaking seeks to present in its entirety the surviving evidence, literary and archaeological, for the Oriental cults. My debt to Professor Vermaseren's work as editor and writer is evident.

I have not listed the primary literary sources. The ancient writers most concerned with these subjects are Plato, Philo Judaeus, Plutarch, Apuleius, Plotinus, Porphyry, Iamblichus, Sallust, Proclus, the Emperor Julian, and the anonymous writers of the Orphic Hymns, the Chaldaean Oracles, the Corpus Hermeticum, the Apocrypha and the Nag Hammadi texts. To these must be added as secondary sources the Christian Fathers whose writings include information on Gnosticism and other esotericisms, particularly Origen and Clement of Alexandria.

In my work of interpretation I have drawn on readings in comparative religion and occult philosophy which have little or no direct bearing on the subject, but which, together with information gained by word of mouth, is essential for the syncretic understanding I have sought. Works on art and architecture have also been invaluable.

Besant, Annie, *Esoteric Christianity*, London, 1901.

Bonner, C., *Studies in Magical Amulets*, Ann Arbor, 1954.

Brown, Peter, *The Making of Late Antiquity*, Cambridge, Mass., 1978.

Browning, Robert, *The Emperor Julian*, Berkeley, 1976.

Campbell, Leroy, *Mithraic Iconography and Ideology*, Leiden, 1968.

Carcopino, Jérôme, *Aspects Mystiques de la Rome Païenne*, Paris, 1942.

——, *De Pythagore aux Apôtres; Études sur la Conversion du Monde Romain*, Paris, 1956.

Cumont, Franz, *The Oriental Religions in Roman Paganism*, Chicago, 1911.

——, *Lux Perpetua*, Paris, 1949.

Dart, John, *The Laughing Savior*, New York, 1976.

Ferguson, John, *The Religions of the Roman Empire*, London, 1970.

Festugière, A., *Hermétisme et Mystique Païenne*, Paris, 1967.

Gersh, Stephen, *Iamblichus to Eriugena*, Leiden, 1978.

Glueck, Nelson, *Deities and Dolphins*, Toronto, 1965.

Gorman, Peter, *Pythagoras, a Life*, London, 1979.

Grant, Frederick C. (ed.), *Hellenistic Religions: the Age of Syncretism*, New York, 1953.

Griffiths, J. Gwynn, *The Isis Book*, Leiden, 1976.

Hanfmann, George M.A., *The Season Sarcophagus in Dumbarton Oaks*, Cambridge, Mass., 1951.

Holland-Smith, John, *The Death of Classical Paganism*, London, 1976.

Jonas, Hans, *The Gnostic Religion: the Message of the Alien God and the Beginnings of Christianity*, Boston, 1958.

Kakouri, Katerina, *Dionysaika: Aspects of the Popular Thracian Religion of Today*, Athens, 1965.

Kerényi, Carl, *Dionysus: Archetypal Image of Indestructible Life*, Princeton, 1976.

Lacarrière, Jacques, *The Gnostics*, New York, 1977.

Levi, Doro, *Aion*, Boston, 1944.

L'Orange, H. P., *Studies in the Iconography of Cosmic Kingship*, Oslo, 1953.

Mead, G. R. S., *Orpheus*, London, 1965.

——, *Thrice-Greatest Hermes*, London, 1906.

Nock, Arthur Darby, *Essays on Religion and the Ancient World*, Oxford, 1972.

Rostovtzeff, Michael I., *Mystic Italy*, New York, 1927.

Teixidor, Javier, *The Pagan God*, Princeton, 1977.

Toynbee, Arthur (ed.), *The Crucible of Christianity*, London, 1969.

Vermaseren, Maarten J., *Cybele and Attis*, London, 1977.

——, *Mithras, the Secret God*, London, 1963.

Vidal, Gore, *Julian*, New York, 1962.

Whittaker, Thomas, *Macrobius*, Cambridge, 1923.

Willoughby, Harold R., *Pagan Regeneration*, Chicago, 1929.

Witt, R. E., *Isis in the Graeco-Roman World*, London, 1971.

Photographic Acknowledgments

Alinari xi, xii, xvi, 2, 5, 24, 25, 31, 37, 46, 55, 57, 74, 79, 85, 90, 92, 95, 101, 107, 119; Alinari/Anderson i, iii, v, 1, 12, 14, 23, 36, 81, 91, 124; Badisches Landesmuseum Karlsrühr Bildarchiv 69; Bagatti, Father O. B. 53; Böhm, O. 56; Clayton, Peter 42; Collart, Professor Paul 120; Deutsches Archäologisches Institut, Istanbul 131; Deutsches Archäologisches Institut, Rome 7, 10, 16, 17, 45, 70, 114, 121; École Française d'Archéologie, Athens 84; Forschungsarchiv für romische Plastik, Universität zu Köln 38; Fototeca Unione, Rome xiii, 39, 78; Giraudon 43, 82, 133, 141; Hirmer 48, 62, 83, 112; Istituto Centrale per il Catalogo e la Documentazione, Rome 27, 109; Maré, Eric de 28, 30, 105; Unesco 50; Warburg Institute, London 4; Yale University Art Gallery 47, 68, 71

Index